Business Etiquette
for the New Workplace

The Results-Driven Manager Series

The Results-Driven Manager series collects timely articles from *Harvard Management Update, Harvard Management Communication Letter,* and the *Balanced Scorecard Report* to help senior to middle managers sharpen their skills, increase their effectiveness, and gain a competitive edge. Presented in a concise, accessible format to save managers valuable time, these books offer authoritative insights and techniques for improving job performance and achieving immediate results.

Other books in the series:

A Timesaving Guide

THE RESULTS-DRIVEN MANAGER

Business Etiquette for the New Workplace

• • •

Harvard Business School Press

Boston, Massachusetts

Library of Congress Cataloging-in-Publication Data

The results-driven manager: business etiquette for the new workplace.
    p. cm. — (The results-driven manager series)
    ISBN 1-59139-974-2
    1. Business etiquette.   2. Management.   3. Etiquette.   I. Harvard
Business School Press. II. Series.
HF5389.R47 2005
395.5'2—dc22

                                                        2005020531

The paper used in this publication meets the requirements of the
American National Standard for Permanence of Paper for Publications
and Documents in Libraries and Archives Z39.48–1992.

Contents

Contents

Choosing the Right Communication Channel

Negotiating When Emotions Run High

Introduction

· · ·

Every day, you probably find yourself wondering how to handle a communications-related issue regarding business etiquette. Some of these issues might seem relatively innocuous—such as "Is this joke appropriate as a starting point for my presentation?" or "Should I use e-mail, a phone call, or a face-to-face meeting to apologize to my marketing counterpart for not being able to support his new proposal?"

Other business-etiquette issues may have seemingly far more crucial ramifications. For example, how much information about your company's financial situation, and what kind of information, should you share with employees and peers who ask about it? What should you do when members of the media contact you for information about a crisis that your organization is enduring? And how much, if at all, should you gloss over problems while motivating your troops to embrace a major change initiative?

Business negotiations present another crop of etiquette dilemmas. For instance, what should you do if you find yourself locking horns with an abrasive or angry counterpart during a negotiation? How appropriate is it to use veiled threats during a bargaining session to get your way? And is it more effective to present a confident demeanor during a negotiation—or a modest one?

The Price of a Misstep

Missteps in any situation calling for the right business etiquette—even in apparently benign circumstances where your intent is good—can severely damage your reputation and effectiveness as a manager. Gaffes can even hurt your unit or company as well. Consider, for example, the story of a CFO who lied to members of other departments about the organization's financial health in order to maintain required confidentiality. He meant well—but instead of lying, he should have said, "I can't provide all the information you're requesting now." The consequences of his misstep? The company's comptroller, a talented young man who knew about the lie, began to doubt the CFO's sincerity. He started looking for a new job with a boss whose intentions he could trust. The CFO's decision to lie thus cost the company a valuable employee.

Another manager unwittingly escalated tensions in her department by using humor inappropriately. Her group had worked a long, hard day on an important project, and the vendor charged with delivering a crucial file that day—a rep from a company in Italy—had failed to show up in time to enable the group to meet its deadline. The manager and her team were as stressed as they'd ever been. In a misguided attempt to relieve the tension, the manager told a joke about Italian businesspeople. An ugly pall settled over the office, and everyone became too irritated by the manager's gaffe to concentrate on finishing the project.

The Advantages of Mastering Business Etiquette

As the above anecdotes reveal, a manager's lack of understanding about business etiquette can have devastating consequences. By contrast, knowing how to use skill and good judgment to resolve a business etiquette dilemma can win you important gains:

- You build a reputation for trustworthiness and tact.

- You send the message that you respect others, and thus you earn their respect in return.

- You become known as a leader who works constructively with others and who forges positive, mutually beneficial relationships with people throughout your organization.

- You motivate your direct reports to perform at their best—whether that means striving to excel in their jobs, embracing needed change, or going the extra mile during tough times.

Clearly, mastering business etiquette generates valuable results—for you *and* your organization. But how should you go about honing your etiquette skills? It isn't easy. After all, in today's increasingly culturally diverse workforces, the chances of saying or doing "the wrong thing" have skyrocketed. A joke that seems perfectly harmless to one person might strike someone else from a different culture as grossly inappropriate. Behaviors that in one society are considered admirable—such as projecting a high level of confidence—might be interpreted as arrogance by people from a different society.

Technological advances have also made it frighteningly easy to unwittingly offend or upset others. Specifically, with the advent of voice mail, cell phones, speakerphone, e-mail, and instant messaging, few of us can be certain of the rules for appropriate use of these various communication channels. In what business settings should you shut off your cell phone, for instance? When is face-to-face communication most appropriate for resolving a conflict? Is it okay to put a caller on speakerphone in your office?

E-mail alone has created a minefield of etiquette dilemmas. One manager, for example, was insulted whenever she received e-mails that did not start with a salutation. She didn't necessarily need a "Dear Ms. Anderson"; she would have been happy with "Hi Toni!" But in her experience, contacting someone without first greeting him or her constituted rudeness. She therefore found it difficult to respect correspondents who violated her code of etiquette. Other e-mail etiquette questions that continue to bedevil businesspeople everywhere include: "Should I spell-check all e-mails before sending them?" "Do I need to include a subject line?" and "Is it all right to express complaints to a colleague in an e-mail?"

With cultural and technological change accelerating, you need to master the principles of etiquette as quickly and thoroughly as possible. That means recognizing and avoiding common etiquette pitfalls, as well as knowing when to express an opinion or share information (and when to keep mum or be evasive). It also means selecting the right communication channel for your message, and using your judgment and communication talents to negotiate successfully.

Challenging goals, all of them. But the articles in this volume will help you. Here's a preview of the techniques, tools, and tips you'll find in this book.

Avoiding Common Etiquette Pitfalls

To avoid common etiquette pitfalls, you need to know what they look like. The articles in this section describe a range of mistakes unwary managers can make. In "Communication Breakdown," the section's first article, executive coach Steve Robbins lays out nine all-too-typical blunders. For example, many managers announce a controversial decision (such as a difficult change initiative) as a done deal, without preparing people one-on-one first and without acknowledging the emotions triggered by the decision. Result? These managers fail to build an alliance around the decision, and uncertainty and resistance reign.

As another prevalent misstep, many managers mix business and friendship communication in one conversation. Friends are supportive, make allowances, and give each other leeway. Managers coach, discipline, and balance their team's needs. If you promise a friend a raise and can't deliver for business reasons, he or she may construe your actions as a betrayal of the friendship.

Writing coach Ken O'Quinn explores another etiquette "don't": the increasing tendency for businesspeople to use convoluted "corporate-speak" to communicate with one another. Unfortunately, the corporate realm is awash in jargon and buzzwords—as evidenced by one executive's memo proclaiming that a newly hired manager would "develop mission-critical cross-platform communications products for multinational financial institutions." Though managers might assume that using such language makes them sound sophisticated or informed, it merely confuses and irritates their audience.

To avoid falling into this trap, choose precise words. For example, instead of saying, "This is the product's functionality," say, "This is how the product works." And resist the urge to pile up modifiers in front of a noun—a habit that forces your listeners to work backward from the noun to discern your meaning. To illustrate, instead of telling your audience about a "business process integration technology," tell them about "technology that helps companies integrate their processes."

In "How Strength Becomes a Weakness," business writer Monci Williams warns against imposing your personal communication style on others—another common misstep among managers. For example, suppose you tend to tell anecdotes and stories in order to communicate a point or convey an insight. This style can be effective in many situations. But perhaps your boss prefers a clipped, "just gimme the headlines" style when receiving information about your business decisions. In this case, your boss may grow increasingly impatient with you and decide that you're an ineffective communicator—and a poor candidate for promotion.

To sidestep this pitfall, watch for symptoms that your dominant style isn't well received—such as bland performance reviews even though you've delivered great results. Practice several other communication styles that will enable you to adapt to others' preferences. And learn to "throttle back" when others' responses to you suggest that you're in "overdrive."

The final article in this section, "Uses and Abuses of Humor in the Office" by business writer Constantine von Hoffman, examines the minefields managers may stumble into while telling jokes in the workplace. For example, do you neglect to learn what your listeners find funny before sharing a joke or humorous story? If so, you risk leaving your audience unmoved, at best—and outraged, at worst.

Indeed, many experts recommend playing it safe by using self-deprecating humor instead of humor aimed at someone else. But be careful to mock a minor aspect of yourself—such as a harmless but foolish thing you did—rather than a major flaw that could reflect poorly on your professional abilities.

Knowing When to Communicate

A core principle of business etiquette is knowing when to share information or opinions with the media, your employees, and other constituents—and when not to. The selections in this part provide helpful guidance.

In "When Not to Speak Up in Public," communications consultant Nick Morgan focuses on whether to answer questions from the press. Morgan challenges the notion that "more communication is always better than less." Sometimes, he maintains, it's "best to keep your mouth shut in public." His advice? During crises, leave it to your company's official spokesperson or communications office to respond to press queries. They're far more skilled at crafting replies that won't inadvertently reveal confidential or damaging information about your organization. Also, avoid talking to the press when your emotions are running high: You're liable to say things you'll regret later.

In "How Much Information Can You Really Share?" business editor Paul Michelman explores strategies for responding to employees who request information about your company that is perhaps best kept confidential. For example, suppose one of your direct reports comes to you and asks whether rumors that your division is being sold are true. You know that a divestiture may be in the offing—but the issue won't be settled for months. What do you do?

The answer depends on numerous factors, and Michelman outlines a series of questions that can help you weigh them. For example, what response to the person's question would enable you to both maintain trust with your direct reports and protect your company's integrity? And what are your company's policies about disclosing high-level corporate information?

The third article in this section—"Debriefing Michael Feiner: Make Conflict Drive Results," based on an interview by Lauren Keller Johnson with the business author—explores the question of when to intervene in a workplace conflict. For example, it may be best to ignore an interpersonal conflict between two members of your team if you believe that the problem will eventually blow over without causing lasting damage. However, under other circumstances, it may be more appropriate to use confrontation to defuse a destructive conflict. To illustrate, Feiner suggests that "if you see two people from different departments locking horns over money or power, you'll be doing them a favor if you confront one or both of them. Point out that the conflict isn't just bad for the business—it's destructive to the person's credibility and career. If handled delicately, this can be enough to persuade people to set their personal agendas aside."

The final article in this section—"Debriefing Lynn Sharp Paine and Elliot Schrage: Managers, Ethics, and Compliance" by business writer Eric McNulty—examines the new disclosure requirements that have come with the Sarbanes-Oxley Act and other legal measures prompted by the recent rash of corporate scandals. Through interviews with Paine and Schrage, McNulty recommends steps for ensuring compliance with the new mandates.

For example, embrace the *spirit* as well as the letter of regulations and compliance standards. After all, much of what occurred at Enron may have been legal, but managers pushed the envelope too far—ultimately destroying the company. Also seek opportunities to talk about values and accountability with your peers and direct reports, rather than waiting for a lapse to force you to address the topic.

Choosing the Right Communication Channel

Choose the right channel for communicating a message to someone else, and you boost your chances of gaining the cooperation and support you need from that person.

Select the wrong channel and you risk offending, confusing, or irritating your audience.

How to match the medium to your message? The three articles in this section provide helpful guidelines. In "Turn off That Cell Phone!" etiquette author Peter Post offers valuable tips. For example, if you've invited multiple people separated by geography to participate in a conference call to make a business decision, put them on speakerphone when they call in. But be sure to introduce each participant and inform them that you're putting them on speakerphone before you start. Post also warns against using e-mail for personal correspondence in the office: The risk that you'll accidentally send the message to everyone in the company—rather than the one recipient you intended—is too high.

Business writer David Stauffer provides additional recommendations in "Can I Apologize by E-Mail?" Different communication channels, Stauffer explains, offer different degrees of personalization. In selecting a channel, consider how much you want to "humanize" your message. For example, if you owe someone an apology, delivering it in person is best, since face-to-face communication is most intimate and enables you to express your sincerity through body language and voice tone as well as words. If an in-person exchange isn't possible, choose a phone conversation. Barring that, use a handwritten note.

If you decide to communicate an emotional or sensitive message through e-mail, combat this medium's notorious impersonal quality by expressing your feelings in two or more different ways. For example, make liberal use of words such as "please" and "thank you," "I'm happy to report," and "I'm pleased to tell you." That way, you reduce the risk that the person reading your message will hear a tone in it that you didn't intend.

In "Don't Push That Send Button!" business writer Nick Morgan provides additional recommendations for using e-mail effectively. For example, select e-mail only when it's the most efficient channel for your need. E-mail is best for short, informal messages that need to be written and read. Messages that don't meet those criteria should be handled through other channels, such as face-to-face or phone conversations. Also avoid e-mail if your message must be error-free. Why? It's much more difficult to proofread text on a computer screen than to proof on the printed page. Thus your chances of sending a message containing typos and other errors soar when you use e-mail.

Negotiating When Emotions Run High

During workplace negotiations—whether you're forging a major business deal or trying to persuade your boss to approve a new program—attention to etiquette becomes particularly crucial. Make a misstep, such as escalating emotional tension or aggressively holding your ground, and you risk losing your bargaining edge or, worse, watching your carefully crafted deal go south.

The articles in this section offer helpful advice for avoiding this scenario. In "When Life Gives You Lemons: How to Deal with Difficult People," negotiations expert Susan Hackley describes strategies for handling those prickly, negative people we seem to inevitably encounter during business negotiations. Hackley's advice includes looking for ways to help the other person save face, a strategy that can make your opponent feel that "I'm getting my way after all." Also disarm your counterpart by showing that you're trying to understand his or her point of view. Ask questions and show genuine curiosity. Another powerful technique is to resist the urge to get angry or give in. Instead, "take yourself mentally to a place where you can look down objectively on the dispute and plan your response."

In "Staying with No," communications consultant Holly Weeks provides additional advice for being heard and respected even when you have to decline a request from your boss, associates, or direct reports. Not surprisingly, saying no to higher-ups can present a particularly daunting dilemma. How you handle yourself can make or break your chances of preserving that relationship. To avoid being maneuvered by your boss into saying yes to an unreasonable request, give the weightiest reasons for your refusal up front. If you start with lightweight reasons, your boss will "swat them away because they aren't very persuasive."

Another technique is to know precisely which persuasion tactics you're most vulnerable to. Do tears move you to give in? What about an ominous suggestion, such as "The union will hear about this"? By knowing your vulnerabilities, you can continue holding your ground even when your opponent applies a full-court press to sway you.

As an additional negotiation pitfall, many managers go into a negotiation overconfident in their ability to "win." In "Great Expectations," Max Bazerman warns us that though confidence is a valuable trait, excessive quantities of it can spawn serious business problems. For example, a company's legal counsel feels 90 percent confident that his firm will win a multimillion-dollar lawsuit. If he emphasizes the possible positive outcome and underplays the fact that the firm will go bankrupt if he loses the case, he'll most likely push ahead with a court date rather than recommend an out-of-court settlement. He'll thus put his company at grave financial risk.

To combat overconfidence during a negotiation, assess your opponent's offer and position as objectively as possible. Simple awareness of the existence and consequences of overconfidence can help you work toward objectivity. Also, before any negotiation, seek out data that could lead you to revise your plans. When you face up to your bargaining weaknesses, you increase the odds of proposing an offer that's acceptable to the other side.

Knowing when to express emotions during a negotiation—and what kinds of emotions to express—presents another dilemma for managers. Business professor Margaret Neale offers guidelines for resolving this question in "Emotional Strategy." According to Neale, bargainers can use emotional expression strategically during different phases of negotiation.

For example, "a positive mood leads to greater value creation" (generating creative ideas for striking a mutually beneficial deal). For this reason, it's helpful to express warmth and friendliness early in a negotiation, "when value creating is most likely to occur." But studies show that negotiators make more concessions when facing counterparts who express anger (even if they don't necessarily *feel* angry). Therefore, consider expressing more negative emotions in the later stages of a negotiation, when parties tend to move from creating value to claiming it.

Management professor Adam Galinsky and researcher Katie Liljenquist explore the strategic use of negative emotions during negotiation in "Putting on the Pressure: How to Make Threats in Negotiations." Making a threat during a bargaining session (for example, a manager tells her boss, "I'll look for a job elsewhere if conditions don't improve here") can evoke negative feelings in the other side. But studies reveal that people evaluate their counterparts more favorably when the counterparts combine promises with threats rather than extend promises alone. Indeed, the threat of experiencing an undesirable outcome seems to motivate cooperation.

But threats can backfire if they're used carelessly. To apply them judiciously, know when to make a threat— for example, when a negotiation has reached an impasse.

Also make them "WISE." A WISE threat expresses your *w*illingness to follow through with what you've threatened to do if your opponent doesn't work to craft a mutually satisfying solution. It also satisfies your and the other side's *i*nterests. In addition, it allows you to *s*ave face—to survive the negotiation with your pride intact. Finally, it is *e*xact—it expresses unambiguous contingencies.

As you've seen, handling ethical dilemmas in the workplace requires a broad range of skills. As you read the selections in this volume, start formulating ideas for how you can enhance your skills. For example, ask yourself:

- "What are the common etiquette pitfalls I'm most likely to fall into? Do I tend to use corporate-speak instead of clear, concrete language? Do I impose my communication style indiscriminately on others? Do I use humor inappropriately? What steps can I take to avoid the pitfalls I'm most vulnerable to?"

- "In what types of workplace situations would it be best for me to speak up? In what situations should I remain mum? For example, should I answer questions about my company from the media? Should I intervene in an interpersonal conflict between two of my team members?"

- "What steps can I take to always select the right communication channel while addressing an etiquette dilemma? When should I use e-mail? Voice mail? A face-to-face conversation?"

- "How can I best handle the dilemmas that arise during workplace negotiations—such as encountering frustration or anger on the part of my opponent, or saying 'No' to my boss?"

By practicing the techniques and using the tools described in this volume's articles, you'll sweeten the odds of avoiding etiquette "don'ts" and handle the most delicate workplace situations with style and aplomb. You *and* your company will benefit.

Avoiding Common Etiquette Pitfalls

• • •

To avoid common etiquette pitfalls, you have to know what they look like. And these pitfalls abound in the business arena. The articles that follow describe the wide range of mistakes unwary managers can make—and ways to sidestep them.

Pitfalls include imposing a controversial change initiative on people without preparing them first and without acknowledging the emotions triggered by change, mixing business and friendship "talk" in one conversation, using convoluted "corporate-speak" in an attempt to impress others, imposing your communication style indiscriminately on others, and using humor inappropriately in business settings. You'll find additional etiquette "don'ts" throughout the selections in this part.

Communication Breakdown

Nine Mistakes Managers Make

• • •

Stever Robbins

How can management communications be screwed up? Let us count the ways. Some, of course, can be traced to the idiosyncracies of leaders—Howard Hughes, for example, who, because of his deathly fear of germs, communicated with employees solely by notes or by telephone. But then there are the common foul-ups that every company falls prey to at one time or another. Here we present nine typical blunders and how to avoid them.

Communicating without Ground Work

Any controversial decision can engender scheming, plots, and politics. So rather than announcing a controversial decision to an entire group, prep people one-on-one. Learn who will object, and why. You can build an alliance around the process, even if you disagree about the content.

Topics about change are the most charged—reorganizations, changing goals, and the departure of key employees create uncertainty, and uncertainty is scary.

One way to cope is to name the emotion. "This reorganization is scary." Then address the concerns. Is the audience uncertain about the future? Share the scenario you expect to unfold. Did a resignation jeopardize a project? Share plans for keeping it afloat. Demonstrate with your voice and body that you get it. You can address emotion better with body language than with words. Rehearse your delivery and make sure you convey concern and empathy.

Lying

Some lies are well-intentioned. Certain topics must remain confidential while they're under discussion. But be careful how you keep secrets. If people know you've lied, you will lose their trust forever. A start-up company's controller watched the CFO lie to members of other departments and subsequently began to doubt the CFO's sincerity. He began looking for a new job with a boss whose intentions he could trust. Lying cost the company a valuable employee.

Rather than lie, train yourself to respond, "No comment" or "I can't answer that fully right now" when asked about these topics. Consistency is important. Warren Buffett never discusses his investments, even with shareholders. As a result, his silence on a particular deal gives away nothing.

Believing That Words Can Overcome Actions

We want to believe that logic and discussion are the stuff of persuasion, but in the end, actions win every time. If you say you value everyone equally, but the executives have reserved parking places near the entrance, the message is clear: status and title matter. If you say you want feedback but explode when the feedback is negative, the message is clear: you only want to hear about the good stuff. Before communicating standards of behavior, values, or goals, look carefully in the mirror. Review your recent decisions, and ask whether the decisions support the values you're espousing. If not, change your behavior. And make sure your reward structure reflects your goal—one company tried to create a culture which embraced best practices from outside while giving a bonus for new inventions and nothing for off-the-shelf solutions. No amount of pleading changed the culture. The bonus sent a stronger message.

By anticipating a mismatch between words and deeds, you can soften the impact. A CEO of a fledgling Internet company knew her month of maternity leave might send the wrong message about her commitment to the company. Two months of planning let her raise the issue with her employees, make her expectations clear, and bring in managers to set the work pace in her absence.

Ignoring the Realities of Power

Surprised that you never hear bad news until it's too late? Don't be. The more power you have, the less you'll hear problems. It's human nature; low-level problems are filtered and softened as they pass up a hierarchy, as each messenger seeks to soften the blow. If you want an honest assessment of a problem, seek out bad news. Welcome it. And when it comes, appreciate it (visibly!).

Messages are magnified as they travel down the hierarchy. If you look pained during a presentation, everyone will "know" you hated the presentation (or worse—the presenter). No one will think to blame the pastrami sandwich you ate too fast. Jokes are especially dangerous. When the managing director of a consulting firm joked,

"If you're not here Sunday, don't bother coming in Monday," his project team wasn't sure what to do. As one explained, "We all knew he was joking . . . we think."

Put a lid on rumors by using plain, simple language. End meetings by reviewing your reactions and next steps. "I enjoyed your analysis, Chris. The sales trend is disturbing—let's follow up on Wednesday."

Mixing Business and Friendship Communication

Business is business, friendship is friendship. Don't mix them in the same conversation. The interests of a friend and those of a manager do not always coincide. Friends are supportive, make allowances, and give each other leeway. Managers coach, discipline, and balance the needs of a team. If you promise a friend a raise and can't deliver for business reasons, it may be construed as a betrayal of the friendship.

Confine friendship and business interactions to separate meetings. If you must mix them, make the boundary clear. "Let's stop talking business for a minute and just talk as friends." When it comes to contentious topics, keep it 100% business in the office. An executive remarked to a friend at a trade show that a new hire was not only extremely capable, but good-looking as well. Bad move. Even to a friend, such comments at work can hurt credibility or turn into a discrimination lawsuit.

Underestimating
Your Audience's Intelligence

It's tempting to gloss over issues because "people won't understand." Why explain a reorganization when you can simply say, "Here's the new org chart"? But that's a cop-out. Front-line employees may not be masters of organizational design, but they deserve to know the rationale behind changes that affect their lives. If you think your people won't understand, remember it's your job to help them.

Many managers like to gloss over problems when motivating the troops. But if things aren't going well, the troops are probably well aware of the problems. In fact, they've probably known longer than you have. Rather than avoiding the situation, find ways to enlist their skills in finding solutions.

Confusing Process with Outcome

In goal-setting, compensation, and evaluation, it's easy to confuse process with outcome. You promise your team a 10% raise, but then the board caps raises at 5%. You fight like mad to raise the number, and compromise on 7%. But your people don't appreciate it. In fact, they're downright resentful. How could they be so insensitive to all your hard work?

Simple. Your hard work was process, but you promised them a specific outcome. You want them to honor how hard you tried, but they wanted a specific number. Since they didn't get it, they just don't care how hard you worked. You want people to love you for your process, not for your outcomes. But when evaluating others, it's always easier to judge outcomes. Most organizations penalize employees for the wrong outcome, even if they did the right thing. And perversely, others are rewarded for the right outcome, even though they reached it the wrong way.

When setting goals or evaluation criteria, communicate and measure both the outcomes and processes involved. Motivation comes from setting ambitious goals, especially if people are free to choose how to reach them. To build a strong organization, however, evaluation should include effort, learning, and improvement—all process measurements—to reinforce effective behavior.

Using Inappropriate Forms of Communication

Different communication channels work best for different topics. Using the wrong channel can send a message straight to the trash or elevate it inappropriately to emergency level. E-mail is great for conveying information, but don't use it for emotional issues; e-mail messages are too easy to misconstrue. If you're squirming while reading an e-mail, turn off the computer, get up, and deal with the situation in person or by telephone.

> We want to believe that logic and discussion are the stuff of persuasion, but in the end, actions win every time.

Phone calls and face-to-face meetings are boring and inefficient media for disseminating information, but great for discussing emotional topics. You can handle the listener's reaction, and you can use your tone of voice and facial expressions to control your message. "I'm sure you did a great job" could be read sarcastically in an e-mail, but can be delivered sincerely in person with the right voice tone.

Furthermore, some people are listeners, while others are readers. Listeners won't glance at written memos but are great in conversation. Readers generate and read great memos, but conversation goes in one ear and out the other. If you talk to a reader or write to a listener, they won't give the message the attention it needs. Don't be afraid to ask people how they prefer to receive information. Most people know the answer, but if they don't, a little attention will reveal what works best.

Ignoring Acts of Omission

What you don't say may be sending as loud a message as what you do say. If you don't give praise, people get the message they're unappreciated. If you don't explain the rationale behind decisions, the message is that you don't trust them. And if you don't tell people where the company is going, they don't know what to do to help it get there.

When fundraising became the CEO's priority at a distance learning company, he stopped communicating his vision to employees. Since money was on his mind, he did mention financial goals. Eventually, the culture became money-focused, and the vision was lost. An employee approached the CEO after seeing him present at a conference, and told him she had never felt so inspired. He changed his internal communication strategy and discovered that bringing the vision back into conversation did wonders for morale.

By their very nature, mistakes of omission are hard to

uncover. Review your major goals and the communication that's needed to support those goals. If you're not regularly sending the messages you need to send, start now. And ask what message may have been sent by your silence so far. Make sure you're giving people feedback on what to do and what not to do. And be willing to ask people: what messages are you getting from me?

For Further Reading

Difficult Conversations: How to Discuss What Matters Most by Douglas Stone, Bruce Patton, and Sheila Heen (2000, Penguin)

Reprint C0009A

Say It Straight

. . .

Ken O'Quinn

When an executive's memo says the company has hired a new manager who currently "develops mission-critical cross-platform communications products for multinational financial institutions," does anyone really understand what that person does?

A meeting agenda reads: "The purpose of the meeting is to get organized to optimize the design and implementation of corrective action plans that will provide optimal cross-functional leveraging, reduce redundancy, eliminate working at cross-purposes, and ensure effective execution and on-going results." Would you know how to prepare for this meeting?

Making communication needlessly obscure is a hallmark of corporate America. *Leverage, synergies, proactive, vision*—business is awash in jargon and buzzwords, but that is no reason to turn business writing into verbal sludge. Whether you're writing a memo, letter, e-mail, or performance evaluation, you are more informative and persuasive when you convey messages the reader can grasp in one reading. That is the essence of clear writing: immediate understanding.

The excessive use of technical terms and once-fashionable phrases that are stale from overuse produces writing that is boring and often unnecessarily complicated, even for people familiar with the topic. Because

> Many people feel they need to use technical terms to sound authoritative and impress the reader.

people are accustomed to reading and hearing these words, they are what tumbles forth when the writer begins tapping on the keyboard. Many people even feel they need to use such words to sound authoritative and impress the reader. But doing so is more likely to muddle the message and confuse the reader.

To avoid potential misreading, the writer must move the reader from the abstract to the concrete. By using a few simple techniques that emphasize clarity at every step, the careful writer can turn a fuzzy concept into a vivid word picture.

Choose Precise Words

Why use *enhance* when you mean *strengthen* or *improve*? Companies sometimes argue that *strengthen* or *improve* should be avoided because they imply that what the company made last year was substandard. That's silly; American business was built on the principle of continual improvement. Readers know what *strengthen* and *improve* mean, but not everyone would be immediately clear about the meaning of *enhance* given the varied ways that companies use it.

Initiative has become a ubiquitous word, but ask five people what it means and you are likely to get five different answers. Is it a goal? An objective? A plan? A step in a process? People using the word almost always are referring to a program or a project—common words that any reader will grasp. If you mean a plan or a tactic, say so.

You could say that new software is "enhanced with substantial new functionality," or you could say, as a magazine writer did, that the software "is bundled with many new features." The second sentence expresses the same idea as the first, but in language that is more concrete and precise. *Functionality* can almost always be substituted with one of three clearer alternatives: *capability, features,* or *how it works.* A reader will immediately grasp any one of those simpler choices.

Connect to the Familiar

Comparisons and examples clarify meaning by taking the reader from the foreign to the familiar. Dean Larson, a safety manager at a U.S. Steel plant, uses an analogy to explain the concept of adsorption to new employees who are undergoing safety training. Adsorption refers to the accumulation of gases or liquids on the surface of a solid or liquid; Larson explains it's "like beads of water on a freshly polished car."

When someone writes of "big-bandwidth applications, such as Internet video and games," the examples ensure that even non-tech-savvy readers can grasp what big-bandwidth applications are.

Watch Those Modifiers

Another way people muddle meaning is by stockpiling modifiers before a noun, as in this brain twister: *a shore-based, long-range, high-frequency surface-wave radar demonstration system.*

What makes this phrase so difficult to comprehend is that the brain is forced to go to the end of the construction and work backward. It is not just a system but a *demonstration system*. Well, not quite. It's a *radar demonstration system*. And it's a particular kind of radar demonstration system, a *surface-wave radar demonstration system*. And not just any surface-wave radar demonstration system, but one that is *high-frequency, long-range*, and *shore-based*.

> Favoring plain language improves readability by giving writing a conversational tone, and it makes writing more persuasive.

Avoid putting your readers through mental gymnastics. Recast such phrases in more natural, conversational language. *Business process integration technology* becomes *technology that helps companies integrate their processes*. An *air traffic management system* becomes a *system to manage air traffic*.

Get Down to Specifics

The late S.I. Hayakawa, a former U.S. senator and a professor of linguistics and rhetoric at the University of

California, developed what is known as the abstraction ladder. A word at the top of the ladder is the most abstract, in that it has many possible interpretations. A word at the bottom of the ladder is precise.

A person who writes, "I work in communications," could be an occupational therapist, a telephone repair person, a marriage counselor, or a satellite dish installer. Saying, "I work in information technology," begins to narrow the person's meaning but still leaves too much to the reader's imagination.

By becoming more specific, the writer moves down the abstraction ladder, which might look like this:

- Communications

- Information technology

- Computers

- Tech support

- Hardware

- PCs

- Desktops

Sometimes being general is sufficient and even preferable, but generally, the lower we stay on the abstraction ladder, the less ambiguous and more clear we become.

Use Jargon Sparingly

One reason we tend to clog our writing with jargon is that we forget that we speak two languages. On the job, we speak the language of our industry. When we leave the office, we speak the language we have been speaking since we were toddlers, a conversational language consisting of plain, familiar words that the brain processes most easily. We cannot avoid the use of technical terms entirely, but it is essential for clarity that we strike the right balance between the simpler language we already know how to use and industry jargon.

Favoring plain language improves readability by giving writing a conversational tone, and it makes writing more persuasive. The common words of everyday conversation tend to be simpler, shorter, and more concrete, naming specific people, objects, and ideas. Those words connect with readers who often are wary of messages laden with corporate-speak, particularly when they arrive from management.

In his famous essay "Politics and the English Language," George Orwell wrote, "Never use a foreign phrase, a scientific word, or a jargon word if you can think of an everyday English equivalent." It is as applicable today as it was when he wrote it in 1946.

Reprint C0207B

How Strength Becomes a Weakness

• • •

Monci J. Williams

Why do some managers succeed, and others fail? Beginning in the 1980s, researchers at the Center for Creative Leadership began to seek a new, more rigorous answer to that ageless question. Reviewing material from thousands of studies, they identified 67 competencies critical to job performance. These included such skills or attributes as listening, creativity, planning, strategic thinking, and approachability.

Organizational development consultants at the center had also seen high-potential managers who seemed to have all the right competencies but who nevertheless plateaued. These men and women weren't unqualified mismatches who never belonged in their jobs; they were the people others expected to make it to the top. Inspired by the work of Jon Bentz, a personnel specialist who tracked the progress of individual careers at Sears Roebuck across decades, Michael Lombardo and a team of social scientists decided to study "derailment," the clinical term for what the rest of us know as failure.

They found, says Lombardo, "that the absence of a competency isn't what derails people. In general, derailers tend to be suffering from a strength in overdrive." In

> ## "The absence of a competency isn't what derails people."

other words, they discover what works for them, and they use it—and use it, and use it.

The center's research identified 19 strengths that, when relied upon too heavily, were most likely to trip people up. Great interpersonal skills—the ability to put another at ease—can turn out to be deadly in excess if those who have them come to be viewed as slick. Strategic thinking may be important to business planning, but the crack strategist who gets things done around the office by proceeding from a master plan can be seen by colleagues as manipulative. The action fanatic, decisive and "Let's go"-oriented in the extreme, may seem impulsive or disorganized to bosses. To coworkers, he's exhausting because "he confuses everybody to death," says Lombardo, now a principal with the organizational-development consulting firm Lominger Ltd.

Achievers, beware: The unsettling truth is that almost any competency can sabotage us if we rely on it too much. Gloria Henn, an executive coach with Henn & Green & Associates, tells the story of an entertainment industry executive whose habitual reliance on her most valued strength put her on probation with a new boss.

An experienced television and film producer, the woman was asked to build a new film division for her company. She was a storyteller by both nature and trade. So was her old boss. But in a reorganization, the old boss was replaced with a linear thinker—the kind of fellow that creative types call "suits." She and he were soon at loggerheads. He wanted bullet points; she told stories. He thought she couldn't communicate effectively, and grew increasingly impatient each time she launched into her storytelling mode in meetings. Newly responsible for the division, he knew he needed the woman, and her creativity, so he asked her to work with a coach.

Ultimately, with the coach's help, the woman and her boss made a pact to compromise on styles and expectations. She would communicate in a clipped, "just gimme the headlines" style when summaries and business decisions were involved. When she was explaining how she arrived at decisions in her more conceptual work, she could use stories. For his part, the boss made a commitment to appreciate how integral her creativity was both to her sense of herself and to the company's success.

> ## "When you're in overdrive, the solution is always to throttle back."

Most overdrivers are not so fortunate. Often the skill that's getting them into trouble has been too important to the company for anyone to try to help them moderate their behavior. That's why overdrivers derail.

What, then, is an overdriver to do? There are standard remedies. The first is awareness. (As the gurus of personal growth like to say, "Awareness, acceptance, adjustment.") Some possible calls to wake up: If your performance is great but your performance reviews are bland, you may be stuck in overdrive. Ditto if you're doing fine with the assignments you have, but you're not getting the assignments you want.

Frustration with being stuck drove Jane Schenck, then a training and development manager with a large service company, to an examination of how her competencies got in her way at work and at home. Schenck was a consummate logician, armed to the teeth with planning skills. But people, she continually found, didn't operate according to her plans—"not my husband, not my kids, not the people I worked with," she says. "When it came to the emotional realm, I didn't understand how people's feelings worked. I was really blind to the richness of people." In recognizing herself as the overpowering force fueling the downward trajectory of her career, Schenck had "a major revelation." It took her almost three years to turn her career around.

Companies in Overdrive

In his 1990 book, *The Icarus Paradox,* Danny Miller cites example after example of companies that go wrong by institutionalizing the strength that made them great in the first place. This "corporate monomania," as Miller, a business professor, describes it, is the reason that "the most dramatically successful organizations are so prone to failure." Harking back to the myth of Icarus—a tale of strength in excess if ever there was one—Miller recounts how companies' victories and strengths "often seduce them into the excesses that cause their downfall. Success leads to specialization and exaggeration, to confidence and complacency, to dogma and ritual."

And so ITT, the aggressive conglomerator, "amplifies" its acquisition strategy until it becomes a kingdom

The overdriver needs to know when to turn his strength off, when to turn it on, and how to let it flow just so much. Schenck gradually learned to gear down, "protect others from my enthusiasm," and seek consensus for her ideas. In the process, she earned the trust of her company's senior executives, who increasingly called upon her to help solve organizational problems. Later, with the support of her bosses, Schenck used this work as an internal consultant to build her own organizational-development consulting firm. Now, seven years later, she has achieved the kind of perspective on her past behavior that perhaps only distance and new success can bring:

of fiefdoms burdened with unmanageable debt. Digital Equipment, known for the engineering of its minicomputers, becomes "an engineering monoculture." And the customers' need for smaller, more economical, more user-friendly products is ignored.

These companies, says Miller, turn into their "evil twins," ineffective and unprofitable "caricatures of their former selves." That a billion-dollar corporate behemoth should fall victim to the same sort of mechanism that derails individuals may seem, to those steeped in the more quantitative aspects of management science, a soft-headed explanation of events. But an organization's most elemental component is the human being. The microcosm is what the macrocosm becomes.

"You think nobody knows. You think you're covering. You're not."

Once they've achieved the requisite awareness, over-drivers should get into the career management analog of a cross-training exercise program. Stretch. Move out of the comfort zone. Use those muscles that may have atrophied. Reading alone won't do the trick; nor will seminars or mere coaching. Complex skills, Mike Lombardo notes, are developed experientially.

The best stretch comes with a new job, preferably in another company. If that's not possible, overdrivers may benefit by expanding or shifting the tasks that come with the job they have. Crisis junkies will grow the most in jobs that involve planning. "Newness—things we're not up to, that's what forces us to develop," says Lombardo.

Novel situations may, of course, make overdrivers insecure, and thus more likely to resort to the strength they've come to rely on. So keeping a hand on the throttle is important. "When you're in overdrive, the solution is always to throttle back," says Schenck. The trick is to develop the "'just-right amount' of the competency that got you this far."

Finding the "just-right amount" is, however, no carefully titrated prescription. So in his current consulting work, Lombardo counsels people to adopt a mental stance of old-fashioned consideration. The idea, touchingly pre-modern, is that we all have a responsibility to wield our greatest talents with courtesy. More hardnosedly post-modern is the fact that—at least in some situations and cultures—courtesy works. "When you have strengths, you have to protect others from those strengths," Schenck says.

The ancient Greeks would say overdrivers, whether corporate or individual, suffer from a tragic flaw called hubris. Most certainly they lack what the Greeks called *sophrosyne*, balance in all things. But it's precisely that balance that, finally, may be the key to sustained success.

Reprint U9612D

Uses and Abuses
of Humor
in the Office

• • •

Constantine von Hoffman

You know the moment too well: It's been a long, tough day on a long, tough project. The vendor hasn't delivered and the deadline has been moved up. You can't imagine survival. You and the staff are as stressed as stressed can be. Inevitably one of two things occurs: Someone makes a nice, gallows-humor-type joke about how the vendor and the deadline should be taken out and shot and everyone laughs and work continues at its normal pace. Or someone tells a dumb blonde joke or a joke about an

Italian, an Hispanic, and a Polish person using not quite those words and an ugly pall settles on the office and now everyone is really too irritated to concentrate on finishing the project anyway.

"Humor is like prescription medicine," says Regina Barreca, a professor at the University of Connecticut and author of *They Used to Call Me Snow White . . . But I Drifted: Women's Strategic Use of Humor.* "It's perfect and wonderful and just the right thing when used in just the right place and in just the right dosage. But it can be toxic when it's used badly."

No office or employee can survive without a sense of humor. But being consistently "unfunny" can be as damaging to your reputation as failure in any other form of social interaction. And in this litigious age it's not just your ability to remember a punch line that goes on trial when you tell a joke.

So what do you do about it? Here are some simple guidelines to what is appropriate in office humor and a couple of pointers that can make even the most humorless among us seem a little funnier.

First, don't make the mistake of assuming that just because you think something is hilarious everyone else will. "Humor is not universal," says Barreca, pointing to one easy distinction between what men and women think is funny: "No woman likes *The Three Stooges.* But women think men behave hysterically when they're sick. Men don't think they're funny when they're ill, they think they're creatures of tragedy."

Dr. John Morreall, a consultant and author of *Humor Works,* says humor can be divided into that which excludes or includes all the members of the audience. "[You need to ask] is this something everyone can feel a part of or does it draw a line down the middle. . . . [There's] humor that's based on competition and divi-

> ". . . Kidding ourselves and kidding each other is a way of showing support for each other. That keeps the organization going and keeps spirits up. It doesn't make people feel outside of the group."

siveness and humor that is based on cooperation. For example, you've got sarcasm and put-down humor on the one hand and kidding on the other."

Morreall says exclusive humor "is pretty traditional and is about someone rising up above another person."

Not surprisingly, Barreca and Morreall put all sexist and racist jokes squarely into the excluding camp.

This hardly cuts down on your humor options, says Morreall. Inclusive humor is based on when "we're all sharing a problem and we're all faced with how much of a pain it is. . . . Kidding ourselves and kidding each other is a way of showing support for each other. That keeps the organization going and keeps spirits up—that's inclusive: It doesn't make people feel outside of the group." Barreca agrees: "When you laugh together you're standing on the same territory."

But remember that different people react to kidding in different ways, says Barreca. "Men will harass each other as a way of being affectionate," she notes. "Joe will say, 'Yo, Bobby—you've been wearing the same suit since 1974.'" And Bobby will know it's Joe's way of saying, 'Hi! How are you?' But if it were Roberta—Roberta would not laugh. She would lock herself in the bathroom until she can order new clothes from a catalog. Women take personal remarks personally."

Also, don't use humor as a way to express other feelings. "A lot of what passes for laughter in the office is veiled hostility," says Matt Weinstein, an author and director of Play Fair. "People don't have the guts to say [some things] straight out. When it's in the guise of a joke, you aren't supposed to take it personally."

So pay attention to the first rule of comedy, which is the same whether you're in a conference room or a comedy club: KNOW YOUR AUDIENCE. The better you know your audience, the more accurately you can gauge what they think is funny. "People you're talking to have to identify with what you're talking about—regardless of what it is," says Jimmy Tingle, a nationally known comic who has appeared on the *Tonight Show* and regularly does presentations to corporations.

Tingle learned this lesson early: Trying out material on an audience he thought he knew pretty well—his mother and father—he dressed up like the Blues Brothers and, harmonica in hand, performed a song called "The Pooper Scooper Blues." The response was clear and direct: "My father looks at me and says, 'Jim, I'm a man who likes to laugh. *The Flintstones* is funny. *McHale's Navy* is funny. That's not funny.'"

And if you aren't dead certain of your audience? Barreca suggests this rule of thumb: "How is this going to sound if someone repeats it to someone who doesn't work in the same place?" She thinks you should assume the person it is being repeated to is the most critical of audiences, "like maybe a lawyer who used to be a nun."

Even if your humor doesn't directly insult a person, if you fail to identify with your audience, you're sunk. Morreall tells of one executive talking to a group of employees during a time of budget cuts and saying that things had gotten so bad that John—an executive VP—was having to give up his corner office and move to a cubicle. As the audience was entirely composed of cubicle dwellers the humor was missed. This is a perfect example of another of Morreall's guidelines: never accentuate your position or your power. Henry Ford was famous for settling disagreements with employees by taking them outside and saying, "Whose name is on the building?" While Mr. Chrysler and Mr. General Motors would have gotten a laugh out of that one, it is doubtful anyone else would have.

If other people's gender and ethnicity are forbidden, what *can* you joke about? Try looking in the mirror. "Self-deprecating humor will usually save the day," says Matt Weinstein. Morreall agrees: "It disarms the audience. Once you've criticized yourself people won't jump on you. It's a distraction." He points to a famous incident when, in a debate, Abraham Lincoln was accused of flopping on an issue and being two-faced. Lincoln, who was considered very ugly in his day, looked at the audience and said, "If I had two faces would I use this one?"

But while making fun of yourself is to be encouraged, trashing yourself is not. So what's OK to mock about yourself? Says Morreall, "When you use self-deprecating humor, pick some minor foolish thing you did, something that happened to you or a feature of your name. . . . If it's something for which you can be indicted or fired, you don't want to bring that up in a joke."

It is even possible for corporations to be self-deprecating. Morreall says that during the 1980s Kodak—which had been renowned for never laying workers off—had to go through several rounds of layoffs. The company circulated a handbill made to look like a movie poster that showed the president and CEO starring in a new movie: *Honey, I Shrunk the Company.*

But, as with anything, there are limits to self-deprecation. Regina Barreca says, "For powerless people, it's not [OK]. If you keep saying, 'I'm such a ditz,' then that's how [superiors] will start to see you. But for the person in power [self-deprecation] is very healthy."

Some other things to avoid when looking about for humor? "Making fun of your spouse or your kids," says Barreca, who adds that she sees a lot of women doing that as a way of being one of the boys. "It is not cool. It reflects badly on you because these are people you either raised or chose. . . . It's a lack of respect. [You need to show] you can make fun of somebody and still respect them."

And the sad truth is there are those among us who just shouldn't try to be funny. Usually there are two reasons for this. One is your sense of humor is just not in sync with everyone else's. They like "Garfield," you like "Zippy the Pinhead," they like *Sleepless in Seattle,* you like *Blue Velvet.* You should be particularly aware of this if you have a very dry or ironic sense of humor. Irony, says Morreall, is the type of humor most subject to misinterpretation. Remember, he adds, "the larger the group you are talking to, the more you've got to shoot for the lowest common denominator of humor. . . . I don't use [irony] with people unless I know them pretty darn well."

The other reason not to try to be funny is the more

you try the less funny you are. "For humor to be successful, it has to be effortless," says Morreall. "If you've been coached and you've been saying the joke over and over . . . even if it's great material, people are going to feel uncomfortable." Morreall says the truth is most people can't tell *jokes*. That's not to say we have a huge humor deficiency, but just that telling *jokes* is hard work. "The big problem with jokes is that every word counts," says Morreall. "A 16-word joke can die if it's stretched to 25 words. And—because it didn't happen to you—[a joke is] harder to remember."

"What I tell people is, most of us can't tell jokes but most of us can tell a story—an event which really happened to you or you can tell like it did," he says. "Try to find one or two stories that make you look amiable, but don't try and put anything subtle into it because then you're crafting it too hard."

Says professional comedian Tingle: "It comes naturally to some people. It's like business, some people have good business sense and some don't. And while you can get good business advice from your father or your brother, if you want to restructure your company, go to a professional."

For Further Reading

A Funny Thing Happened on the Way to the Boardroom: Using Humor in Business Speaking by Michael Iapoce (1988, John Wiley & Sons)

Humor Works by John Morreall (Human Resource Development Press)

Managing to Have Fun by Matt Weinstein (1997, Fireside)

They Used to Call Me Snow White . . . But I Drifted: Women's Strategic Use of Humor by Regina Barreca (1991, Viking)

Reprint C9902A

Knowing When to Communicate

. . .

A core principle of business etiquette is knowing when to share information or opinions with the media, your employees, and other constituents—and when not to. The selections in this part provide helpful guidance.

You'll find advice, for instance, on when to answer sensitive questions about your company from the media and from direct reports and peers. You'll also discover techniques for determining when to intervene in a workplace conflict. Additional strategies include ensuring that your organization complies with new laws (such as the Sarbanes-Oxley Act) that require disclosure of particular company information.

As these selections reveal, that widespread assumption—"the more communication, the better"—is due for reexamination.

When Not to Speak Up in Public

● ● ●

Nick Morgan

It's a common myth that more communication is always better than less. Unless you're in the midst of a media firestorm yourself, you may well believe that old sound bite that "any publicity is good publicity."

But the truth is that there are times when it is best to keep your mouth shut in public, in spite of the deep-seated human need to appear on CNN. An obvious one, for example, is when you have nothing productive to say except "No comment." In the media's eyes, that's as good as a confession of guilt. But beyond the obvious, what about when you're an expert in the midst of a crisis? Shouldn't you spout off in your area of expertise? Or what about some other, less dramatic moments? What are the best times for saying nothing at all? Let's take a few examples from my years of experience as a communications consultant, the expert crisis first. (The situation has been disguised to protect the "media challenged.")

In Times of Crisis, Leave the Heavy Lifting to the Pros

The crisis hit early on a Monday morning. Over the weekend, a reporter found out about a potential recall for the wildly popular new toy the company had been producing as fast as it could. Wall Street responded by taking 30% of the stock value away in the first 20 minutes of trading. Until now, the marketer in charge of the toy had been riding high—the product was an instant smash, and everyone had been calling him the next Toy Genius. But now his phone was ringing off the hook. The press— and the company spokeswoman—wanted him to hold a news conference as soon as possible. The company didn't have a crisis communication plan in place; it was something it always meant to do, but never got around to. So no one was trained, certainly not the hapless marketer. What should he have done?

Well, certainly not what he actually did. He revealed the whole tortured history of the product, unwittingly giving tons of ammunition to the trial lawyers. So when you're up to bat, resist the temptation to play the hero and swing for the information fences. Knowing what to say to the press, and what not to, is difficult under the best of circumstances. Under these conditions, you're liable to say something unintentionally disastrous. Leave it to the spokesperson, unless the recall involves personal injuries. In that case, you'd better hope that your CEO is good in front of the press, because when lives and limbs are on the line, the public needs to hear from the company's upper echelons.

There's a reason why presidents and other really important folks have spokespeople. They can build a rapport with specific members of the press, as well as expertise in the fine art of knowing when to stay on message (almost always) and when to go off (hardly ever). Spokespeople also have an option up their sleeves that non-experts rarely do: the chance to come back for a clarification, because of that ongoing relationship with the press.

What are the other situations where it's best not to stand up and be counted as a public speaker?

Beware the "Briefing"

Presentations are not good venues for conveying large amounts of complex information. Whether it's to the press, internally to your company, to the investor community, or the like, keep your briefings just that—brief. If you've got a lot of information to get across, hand it out in written form. People—even reporters who are trained to take in information—rarely retain much detail from presentations. They are entirely likely to get it wrong.

I once watched what should have been an easy win for a politician go horribly wrong because of the detail problem. The politician had just arrived by helicopter at a disaster area and was asked, "Has this been declared a federal disaster area?" The real answer was "not yet, but soon." But the politician got defensive and began to explain that the state was doing all that needed to be done, and it was just a matter of getting reimbursed by the Feds, something that could be done afterwards, when everyone was once again safe in their beds. No one in the press could retain all the detail. The story that got written was, "State has no plans to declare federal disaster area," a story that created a temporary disaster of its own.

Briefings establish credibility by making a few basic points about the issue or product in question, and then taking a limited number of questions. The speaker should be well briefed beforehand in the right messages and rehearsed in delivery. This is not a natural act, however. The feelings of excitement and adrenaline that go along with public speaking usually cause a kind of hysterical relief to set in after the first few minutes, and many a presenter—even experienced ones like politicians—has given the game away by spilling too much sensitive information and obscuring key messages.

On the Other Hand, Avoid Also the Unutterably Routine

Once a speaking event becomes routine, it's time to question its existence and your presence there. First of all, it's not worth the aggravation of preparing a presentation if no one cares whether you're there or not. Presentations should be reserved for the times when what takes place couldn't happen any other way. Use that as a simple test: ask yourself, could we handle this routine event better with an e-mail, a memo, or through some other means of communication?

The risk is that you'll start treating the regular event as casually as everyone else, and you'll be tempted to wing it. Most people think they're brilliant when they wing it, but the audience usually thinks otherwise. Even the impromptu should be rehearsed, if it's important. And if it isn't important, don't do it.

I once saw a traditional political event that for years had excluded women and minorities become temporarily exciting when a reporter asked one of the speakers what he personally thought of the tradition. The speaker casually replied, "This represents something that should have died out years ago." It was an honest, impromptu, and tactless attempt at humor, and it led to a "nine day wonder" of debilitating media attention that should never have happened, since the speaker was referring to the exclusions, not the event itself. The newspaper headline? "Speaker blasts local tradition." So never, ever wing it. If it's public, it needs practice.

Give No Presentation Before Its Time

Whenever your emotions are running high, try to avoid the podium. You're liable to say things you'll regret later. A presentation is a performance, and while you need to have access to your genuine emotional responses, you'll suffer if you are ruled by them. Remember Senator Ed Muskie on the 1972 campaign trail? His tears in response to spurious allegations about his wife cost him his candidacy in an era when real men couldn't cry. Never respond just because the press is asking you to. You can always take five and huddle with your team to figure out what to say.

You want a warm heart and a cool head when you're speaking in public. If events force a response, then keep it brief and be as responsive as you can within that particular moment. Don't guess, predict, analyze, speculate, infer, or otherwise stray from the immediate, the known, and the concrete. There are times in this era of over-communication when the less said the better.

Reprint C0203E

How Much Information Can You Really Share?

• • • •

Paul Michelman

You look up to find the concerned face of a key employee darkening your door. He's heard rumors that the division might be in trouble, that corporate support is wavering, and that potential buyers are lining up. He wants to know what you know.

Though the rumors are not altogether accurate, they

do contain more than a few grains of truth. In spite of some recent unit successes, the company's board of directors recently gave the department mixed reviews: some directors are dubious about the unit's long-term prospects and are open to acquisition offers; others, however, continue to believe in the unit's promise and want to give it a couple more years to produce bigger things. The issue won't be settled for months.

How Do You Deal with It?

Like so many executives over the past few years, you have made a commitment to internal "transparency"—where not only the numbers but also the big picture is discussed candidly with employees. Your commitment to openness has been largely successful; it has engendered feelings of trust, empowerment, and commitment to both you and the company. It hasn't always been easy: just as bad numbers can send people into states of unfounded pessimism, good data threatens to skyrocket them into false states of euphoria. But, by and large, you've been able to keep your people grounded by helping to develop their strategic and financial wherewithal, by sharing company news and data with a strong sense of the larger context, and by giving your teams a great deal of responsibility for making decisions based on the wealth of information they can now access.

But at this point the news is big and possibly threatening. Worst of all, it's vague. If not well managed, the message could have devastating effects. You've been sitting on what you know for weeks, not sure how or when to share it. You've considered simply waiting for something more definitive—but who knows when that will come? Now your hand has been forced. If one employee has heard rumblings, so have others—maybe customers have heard them, too. Any executive who has made the commitment to this kind of transparency will one day face this dilemma: how do you deal with developments that are utterly and wholly . . . ambiguous?

Living Up to Your Standards

When you get right down to it, what choice do you have? You've made a commitment to openness and reaped substantial benefits by doing so, but now your reputation is on the line. If you don't take the offensive and word gets out on its own (and you know one day it will), you'll destroy all the trust and goodwill you've built.

"To secure the economic benefits of honesty, one must be perceived as being *committed* to honesty, which means viewing truth as something intrinsically good and not subject to reevaluation on a case-by-case basis," writes Harvard Business School professor Lynn Sharp Paine in *Value Shift: Why Companies Must Merge Social and Financial Imperatives to Achieve Superior Performance.* More important, she notes, "Divergences between ethics and financial self-interest that appear acute in the short term can narrow or disappear if a longer-term perspective is taken."

True, Paine's big-picture purview may be a bit hard to swallow when the sharp horns of a dilemma are pressing on your gut, but history proves it time and again: diverge once from the public commitment you've made—especially on a significant issue—and the trust may disappear forever. But there's more to this than just living up to your commitments. If you don't take the offensive

> # How do you deal with developments that are utterly and wholly . . . ambiguous?

on delivering this news, you'll lose any opportunity to present it in the most constructive context.

"People aren't happy when the unexpected happens, but they are even unhappier if they find out you tried to hide it," says Bruce Patton, a partner at Vantage Partners. "Given that something has happened and others will find out, most people judge you and decide what to do based on how you are responding. How clear is your thinking, persuasive your analysis, comprehensive your consideration of alternative explanations and options, and creative and risk-mitigating your response?"

So the question is no longer *what* you do, but *how* do you do it.

Take Cues from Negotiation Strategy

With negative or ambiguous information, "the interests at stake are not necessarily an attempt to persuade or influence," says Danny Ertel, also a partner at Vantage. "They are about being able to manage a business effectively, about being able to make good decisions based on reliable information, about being treated fairly."

To find the right balance in presenting tricky information, Ertel suggests executives consider the following questions, which originate in the realm of negotiation strategy:

WHAT ARE YOUR KEY INTERESTS? In this case, the executive's interests are twofold: maintain a trust-based relationship with her reports and protect the integrity of the business.

WHAT ARE THE INTERESTS OF THE MANY AUDIENCES WHO WILL INVARIABLY HEAR AT LEAST SOME PARTS OF THE MESSAGE? For the unit's managers—the executive's primary concern—the interests probably begin with the stability of their livelihood. They want to know what the future holds for them.

WHAT ARE SOME OPTIONS FOR MEETING THOSE INTERESTS? The options range, of course, from blunt truth-telling to some form of denial, with many variations involving what information is disclosed, to whom, when, and under what conditions. Though the most effective approach will vary by the particulars of the situation and individuals involved, one suspects the right choice lies closer to blunt truth than to denial.

WHAT ARE SOME STANDARDS OF LEGITIMACY? Many possible standards can guide this dialogue: there are, for instance, regulatory requirements about information that can be shared without imposing

Setting the Ground Rules for Transparency

One way to help pave the road for dealing with the type of situation we present here is to set some well-communicated standards up front.

"There are obviously business and competitive reasons that a company can't fully disclose and be completely transparent with its staff," says Heath Shackleford of American Healthways. "But it is the leadership's job to both explain what those areas are and why they are limiting specifics related to those areas."

For example, notes Vantage's Danny Ertel, companies need to limit disclosure of "information that will

corresponding obligations on the recipient; there are practices followed by privately held businesses, family businesses, and employee-owned businesses. Here's the lynchpin: if the answer you provide does not feel truthful and complete, you fail.

Seeking Constructive Legitimacy

In this case, the executive could fulfill her commitments and still protect the business by shifting the focus of the conversation to the future, says Heath Shackleford, manager of public relations at American Healthways.

give competitors a leg up or allow its suppliers to take advantage of a temporary situation."

Leaders should engage in a dialogue with their managers about the kind of information that is appropriate to disclose, Ertel says. "I don't think execs should make blanket commitments to be 'completely open'; I think they should commit carefully to things they can live up to, which may mean a somewhat more subtle approach to discussing information and its implications, at different points in time, with different groups under different ground rules." The dialogue with managers and employees is the critical part: it sets the expectations about what is responsible sharing of information and what is responsible use of that information.

"What the manager really wants to know is what must be done to keep his unit afloat," Shackleford says. "So, first acknowledge there are some concerns and that he is correct in sensing that everything isn't roses right now. Admitting this is safe enough because the manager wouldn't be at the door if he didn't already have a sense of that."

From here, focus on what you can do together to control your destiny and give your reports some ownership of the solution.

"If there are numbers to hit, improvements to make, etc., let him help you. Maybe you need him to help keep morale up in the short term until the storm is over. Maybe you need him to motivate one of the departments under his watch."

If you send people out with some feeling of control over the outcome, Shackleford notes, "it won't matter so much that you couldn't specifically dole out everything you know about the situation."

Reprint U0411C

Debriefing Michael Feiner

Make Conflict Drive Results

• • •

Lauren Keller Johnson

Perhaps you've witnessed it: two managers in your organization go head to head in a grab for power, position, or pay. The conflict seeps down into the departments they oversee, as teams become aware of the contest and start backing their respective leaders. Soon communication and collaboration between the opposing departments break down.

This scenario represents a particularly destructive brand of conflict, says Michael Feiner, a professor at Columbia

University's Graduate School of Business. In other "unhealthy" forms of conflict, employees jockey for favor with the boss, people argue over how they're being treated by the firm, and individuals sabotage one another's professional reputations to advance their own careers.

Whatever shape unhealthy conflict takes, it always wreaks the same kind of havoc: it saps people's concentration and focus, and drains much-needed attention and energy away from the issues that matter most to the organization overall. It also gives conflict a bad name. Executives and managers conclude that all conflict is unhealthy and should be squelched.

But not all conflict is destructive, says Feiner. "Contests over personal agendas are unhealthy, but conflicts over ideas are good." In fact, he says, skilled leaders purposefully encourage debate, disagreement, and discussion over ideas, issues, and important decisions. "The higher the stakes in a key decision, the more vital it is to stimulate this healthy kind of conflict." Battles over ideas, Feiner says, "lead to creativity, innovation, and positive change by squeezing the best ideas from each participant's mind."

The most effective executives know how to minimize the bad conflict while cultivating the good. This balancing act begins by developing a new mindset regarding conflict.

Avoiding a Corporate Coronary

To develop the right attitude for "leading conflict," managers should think of conflict as cholesterol, Feiner says.

"Once you compare the negative impact of bad cholesterol on your health with the benefits of good cholesterol, you'll likely feel more motivated to change the way you're doing things. You adopt whatever discipline and practices—new fitness or dietary regimens—you need to reduce the bad kind and increase the good kind."

Similarly, leaders who are able to recognize the downside of unhealthy conflict and the upside of healthy conflict are better able to manipulate the levels of both varieties. "You save your company from having a corporate coronary," Feiner says.

Handling conflict deftly entails a new attitude toward leadership. "Relying on your power to push people into following you only generates destructive conflict," Feiner says, "because people feel bullied into complying. You want their commitment, not their compliance. You want to pull people—take them with you—not push them. And you need to respect the interdependence inherent in workplace relationships." Managers can begin adopting this new mindset about leadership by asking themselves a simple question: Does the behavior of the people around me suggest that I'm pulling people—or pushing them?

But this alone won't generate effective conflict leadership. Executives must also master the two sets of skills needed to manage each type of conflict.

Minimizing Bad Conflict

When unhealthy conflict rears its head, many executives don't realize they have a range of options for dealing with the situation. Instead, they assume that they have two choices at most: avoiding the conflict or confronting one or more of the parties.

To be sure, each of these responses may have merit under specific conditions. For example, a manager may decide that it's best to ignore an interpersonal conflict between two members of her team if she believes that the problem will eventually blow over without causing lasting damage.

But under other circumstances, it may be more appropriate to use confrontation to defuse a destructive conflict. For instance, Feiner suggests that "if you see two people from different departments locking horns over money or power, you'll be doing them and your company a favor if you confront one or both of them. Point out that the conflict isn't just bad for the business—it's destructive to the person's credibility and career. If handled delicately, this can be enough to persuade people to set their personal agendas aside."

Of course, such conversations can be tricky. Feiner recommends adapting your delivery style to the person you're confronting and emphasizing his interests over the company's interests.

Executives and managers can minimize bad conflict even more skillfully, Feiner says, if they develop options beyond avoidance and confrontation. In *The Feiner Points of Leadership: The 50 Basic Laws That Will Make People Want to Perform Better for You,* he suggests several additional responses:

COMPROMISE. Find a fair solution that satisfies both parties. For example, your company's marketing executive wants to launch a new product on September 1, but the manufacturing executive (who has had long-standing disagreements with the marketing executive) argues for November 1. You encourage them to agree to October 1.

DELEGATION. Ask a subordinate with a strong track record of conflict resolution to address the problem on your behalf. This sends the message that not every contest should escalate up the corporate ladder.

COLLABORATION. Encourage the parties to openly discuss their disagreement and determine a solution—jointly. Start the conversation by acknowledging that the parties have different viewpoints. Then ease intense emotions by guiding the discussion toward an assessment of the facts—through questions such as "What additional data can we bring in to arrive at the best solution?"

Be open about the damage the conflict is causing: "Your differences have created a civil war in the company. How can we resolve this dispute for your own good and the good of the organization?" This option takes time, but it produces the most enduring results.

ACCOMMODATION. Encourage one of the parties to "give in for the sake of keeping the peace." This option can be most useful if maintaining the relationship between the parties is essential and the dispute doesn't seriously jeopardize the organization.

The central point about options, Feiner says, is that the more of them you know how to use, the more flexibility you have in resolving unhealthy conflicts. "When you become aware of a bad conflict," Feiner notes, "simply asking 'What are my options?' can reveal the most appropriate way of responding.

"Notice if you're relying on just one or two options most of the time. If you are, learn how to use the other options. You want a variety of pitches to draw from."

Maximizing Good Conflict

In Feiner's view, the key to healthy conflict is the energetic exchange of ideas. Leaders have numerous tech-

Living with Conflict

Every social system experiences good and bad conflict, Feiner says—and organizations are no exception. "People have always been ambitious and achievement-oriented. These days, the increasing pressure to generate better business results and satisfy Wall Street may be pushing more people to put their own interests over those of their organization. But overall, conflict has

niques at their disposal for stimulating "good cholesterol" debate and disagreement. For example, Feiner encourages executives and managers to avoid stating their opinion on an issue early in a discussion. "You'll only encourage groupthink," he says, "because few people will feel comfortable challenging you. Instead, make sure your opinion is the last one stated."

Another technique involves noticing when one or more participants in the debate have fallen silent. "When you see that happening, ask the person what he or she is thinking and feeling." Feiner also agrees that designating someone to play devil's advocate on an issue can further stimulate a lively or even heated exchange of ideas.

Feiner describes another method known as divergence/convergence: participants privately write on Post-it notes what they consider to be the three key issues in the decision at hand. The notes are arrayed on the wall to reveal where consensus and dissent exist. Through debate and

been a constant in business life." The best leaders don't set out to squelch all conflict. Instead, they understand the difference between healthy and unhealthy conflict and seek to tip the scales toward the good variety. They develop a broad repertoire of options for minimizing destructive conflict. At the same time, they encourage people to check their personal agendas at the door—and argue about ideas instead.

discussion based on the notes, participants then work toward a convergence of opinion. This approach helps ensure that everyone's ideas are included in the decision process.

Such techniques enable a leader to send an important message: "I want your ideas. I want your disagreement. I want you to challenge me." The resulting interaction of ideas provides the foundation for the innovative, creative thinking that healthy conflict generates.

Reprint U0409D

Debriefing Lynn Sharp Paine and Elliot Schrage

Managers, Ethics, and Compliance

• • •

Eric McNulty

Among the clearest messages to come out of the misdeeds and lapses in good judgment that have rocked corporate America in recent years is that responsibility for compliance and ethics can no longer be confined to the boardroom, the general counsel's office, or the HR department. Indeed, these issues are increasingly recognized as core management concerns—and managers who do not embrace their roles in this area do so at their peril.

At many organizations, the specific role of individual managers in ethics and compliance is just beginning to take shape. To better understand the emerging landscape—and how managers at all organizational levels fit in—we sat down with Lynn Sharp Paine, professor of business administration at Harvard Business School, and Elliot Schrage, a lawyer and business adviser at the Council on Foreign Relations. Paine is the author of *Value Shift: Why Companies Must Merge Social and Financial Imperatives to Achieve Superior Performance.* Schrage researches and writes on the social impact of globalization and formerly directed both the social responsibility initiatives and global compliance organization for Gap, Inc.

Beyond Requirements

Legal mandates under the Sarbanes-Oxley Act, the new exchange-listing requirements, and other measures are strict, and enforcement will be vigilant. But more important for managers to understand is that customers' and other stakeholders' expectations have changed, Paine says. "People have shown they prefer to buy from and invest in companies that behave well. The most desirable employees want to work for an organization they can be proud of. It's now not whether you choose between social and financial performance but, rather, to see the two as complementary and leverage them for competitive advantage."

Meeting these new expectations is more difficult than ever. Core business trends, such as outsourcing, strategic alliances, and global supply chains, require a manager to be aware of the actions and policies of an entire network of organizations—not just his own company. Indeed, nongovernmental organizations (NGOs), which have

> Think through the unintended consequences of your compensation and incentive plans.

emerged as a second tier of oversight, will often treat you and your suppliers as one. Therefore, smart companies are holding frontline managers—who have the best view of what is actually happening on the ground—responsible for paying as much attention to the labor, environmental, and financial practices of partners as they do to cost and delivery dates.

"In a time of increasing transparency," says Schrage, "you can't run, and you can't turn a blind eye to what your partners are doing."

How, then, do you implement superior practices? How do you ensure compliance throughout a complex, global supply chain? How do you create common values among a workforce that may number in the hundreds of thousands—many of whom may work for third parties? How do you make all of the effort and investment pay off on the bottom line?

Begin with the Basics

To start with, you have to get the basics right. This varies a lot by industry and the status of the company as U.S. or non-U.S., public or private, and so on. Sarbanes-Oxley has most public companies started toward a deeper understanding of compliance (though many are still discovering its full implications). The important insight for

Concrete Steps Managers Can Take

- Provide adequate, ongoing training and clear, current systems that allow your workers and suppliers to comply as easily as possible. The easier it is to comply, the more likely you will achieve compliance.
- Ensure that those who must comply have access to the right information at the right time by integrating compliance needs into your IT systems.
- Talk about values and accountability regularly.

managers is that governance responsibility extends well beyond senior management.

In a 2000 survey of large-company employees in the United States, half said the misconduct they observed in their company was due to inadequate training. And that survey was done before the additional layers of complexity provided by Sarbanes-Oxley and the new listing requirements.

"You need to make sure that people throughout your organization understand the specific implications of the relevant regulations on the day-to-day operations of their business," says Paine. "Frontline managers can be helpful in spotting gaps and inconsistency in a company's code of conduct," Schrage adds. "A corporate code is only useful if it is specific enough to give people

> Don't wait for a lapse to force you to address the topic.
> - Create incentives that align with social and financial expectations.
> - Embrace the spirit as well as the letter of the regulations and compliance standards. In the end, much of what occurred at Enron may have been legal, but by pushing the envelope too far, managers destroyed the company, evaporated shareholder value, and cost thousands their livelihoods.

real guidance. A policy saying 'we obey the law and adhere to the highest standards'—a common approach—just isn't good enough."

Schrage encourages managers to raise awareness by giving suppliers and customers copies of the code. "Make it clear that you are holding them to the same standards," he says. "The key is to achieve alignment between expectations and execution."

According to Schrage, it also helps to humanize the standards. "I know of one manager for an apparel company who spends a lot of time visiting manufacturers outside the U.S. He imagines his grandmother walking beside him when he visits a plant. If he sees something he would be uncomfortable having her see, he knows he should be concerned. For him, she's the person he can't look in the eye and say, 'Well, but they do it at a lower cost than anyone else.' For you, it might be a spouse or clergyperson, but it doesn't matter—putting a face on the standards makes them harder to ignore."

Communicate and Lead by Example

A 1999 study of Fortune 1000 CEOs found that 62% of them never spoke about ethics in live or taped company communications. "Imagine what would happen to performance if 62% of CEOs never talked about sales or keeping costs in line?" Paine asks. "What the CEO talks about becomes important to the organization."

But frontline managers needn't wait for the CEO, says Paine. By discussing the issues and asking probing questions at the unit and department levels, managers can have significant local impact. Their staff will pay more attention to ethics and compliance when they realize how important it is to their boss.

Don't underestimate the power of mythology. Every company has legends—the plant manager who met a production goal against great odds, the salesperson who landed a huge contract, the upstart who launched a new product—and those legends help shape future behavior. Put those people who make a courageous ethical decision in the spotlight so that their example can be a beacon to others.

Make Compensation Your Ally

Compensation and incentives are predictable drivers of behavior, Paine says. When you see business scandal, you will virtually always find a compensation issue behind it.

Paine cites a situation that Sears Roebuck and Co. faced in the early 1990s. "Mechanics were misleading customers—telling them their cars needed work when they didn't. Why? These weren't all bad people working there, and Sears isn't a fly-by-night company. But the incentive system rewarded mechanics only for short-term revenue generation, regardless of the methods they used. There were no rewards—in fact, there were unintended penalties—if a mechanic looked at a car and deemed that work wasn't necessary or that a quick adjustment would solve the problem."

The lesson? Think through the unintended consequences of your compensation and incentive plans, Paine says. Balance aggressive production goals with measures such as customer satisfaction levels to help ensure that you aren't encouraging behavior that will hurt you later on.

Paine argues that much of the evolution of accountability has been under way for decades. The general expectations for the behavior of private-sector companies have been elevated commensurate with the increased role business now plays in society. She predicts that the intensity related to ethics, governance, and compliance will decrease but that the fundamental shift in accountability is here to stay.

Managers need to understand their new role, says Schrage. "Your job is not what it used to be. Managers now have to be much better at appreciating how decisions impact all stakeholders."

Reprint U0408E

Choosing the Right Communication Channel

• • •

Choose the right channel for communicating a message to someone else, and you boost your chances of gaining the cooperation and support you need from that person. Select the wrong channel and you risk offending, confusing, or irritating your audience.

How to match the medium to your message? The articles in this section provide helpful guidelines. You'll find tips for determining when to put a caller on speakerphone in your office, when to use e-mail versus a phone call or face-to-face conversation, and what the appropriate channel is for apologizing, complaining, and "humanizing" a sensitive or delicate interpersonal communication.

E-mail receives special treatment in this section, owing to its notorious impersonal quality and the difficulty inherent in drafting error-proof messages.

Turn off That Cell Phone!

An Interview with Peter Post

• • •

As great-grandson of Emily Post, Peter Post knows a thing or two about being polite. He and his sister-in-law, Peggy Post, are coauthors of *The Etiquette Advantage in Business: Personal Skills for Professional Success,* which brings to business the same sensible approach that character-izes the classic Emily Post books on social etiquette.

The book comes at a time when lapses in courtesy abound. Contributing writer Richard Bierck interviewed Post on the nature of these lapses and what can be done about them.

What do you view as the biggest problem in business etiquette of late?

POST: Without a doubt, the big new problem is e-mail.

People are getting into trouble because they think of e-mails as private documents. Their e-mails aren't their own; they belong to the company. The classic example is a boss who has a discussion with an employee about work, and the employee types up an e-mail about it, and in attempting to send it to a friend, sends it to everyone in the office, including the boss. Back when we just sent snail mail, people had lots of opportunity to change what they said—and to make sure it was going to the right individuals.

What are some of the more egregious business behaviors during meals these days?

POST: Perhaps the most egregious thing is people using their cell phone during business luncheons and dinners. What's most appalling is that they're not only taking calls, they're making them. I was up at the Burlington Country Club here in Vermont having lunch. In come three guys. The third guy sits down at the table. The two have been waiting for him. All of a sudden, the third guy reaches down into his briefcase, whips out his cell phone, dials up a number, and starts talking. The other two are in shock. Their body language went from being engaged and friendly to arms across, sitting back, looking around the room. The whole tone of that lunch went south.

Not only should you not make calls in such situations,

but you should turn off your phone—and your pager—to give people your full attention.

Another phone-related problem: using the speaker phone. It's just impolite. Not only does the person answering sound as if they're in a conch shell, but the caller doesn't know if other people are in the room. If there are people that you want to include in the conversation, first inform the person who has called you, then introduce them.

How about having the whole conversation on the speaker phone?

POST: As long as you're doing it for a reason—as when multiple people are making business decisions—it's fine. But be sure to introduce people and inform them you're putting them on the speaker phone before you start.

Your book deals extensively with appropriate dress. Is this a problem area these days?

POST: Definitely. I think the confusion comes because of casual dress and dress-down Fridays. People are also sensing that if you get into real casual dress, there's perhaps a little less respect accorded to the manager, and that can lead to confusion and difficulty in the workplace. A study at the University of North Carolina found that casual dress has caused problems for management.

We'd like to believe that people judge us by what we think, but we know that people also judge us by what we wear.

Is the problem that some employees believe they are the same rank as management because they dress the same?

POST: That's right. One of the things that businesses today are promulgating is teamwork. For teams to be able to work together, every member of the team needs to feel that he or she can be a full contributor. So it may be appropriate to wear the same type of clothing. The more casual the atmosphere, the more we need to figure out how are we going to *not* let it cause stress in the workplace.

So would one solution be for managers to try to dress just a shade more formally than their employees, even on casual-dress days?

POST: At companies where the confusion is occurring, that would be a good approach.

People who forget the names of people commonly don't attempt to introduce them at all, fearful that the person will be offended. How should we deal with this one?

POST: This is not rocket science. I went to a meeting the

other day where I was introduced to one of the attendees while riding up in the elevator. So when I started my presentation, I walked over to the person who had been in the elevator with me. I said, "I was just introduced to you a minute ago and I can't remember your name. Could you tell me what it is again?" And she told me her name. There's an example of etiquette: I couldn't remember her name, so I admitted it and I asked her for her name again. Nobody got hurt by that.

For Further Reading

The Etiquette Advantage in Business Personal Skills for Professional Success by Peggy Post and Peter Post (1999, Harper-Resource)

Reprint C0005C

"Can I Apologize by E-Mail?"

• • •

David Stauffer

Have you ever used e-mail to apologize to a coworker? Delivered a reprimand to a subordinate with a voice-mail message? Jetted across the country just to deliver important news in person?

The various communication options at our fingertips today can be good for convenience and productivity—and at the same time very troublesome. With so many ways to communicate, how should a manager choose and use the one that's best—particularly when the message to be delivered is bad or unwelcome news for the recipient?

We've surveyed business communication consultants

and manners mavens to come up with the following guidelines for effectively using the alternative ways of delivering difficult messages.

Choose how personal you want to be.

A face-to-face communication is the most intimate. Other choices, in descending order of personalization: a real-time phone call, a voice-mail message, a handwritten note, a typewritten or printed letter, and—the most impersonal—e-mail and fax. Some of these may switch rank according to the specific situation or your own

> A rash outburst can haunt a career for years—and today's technologies provide whole new avenues for instant oblivion.

preferences; for example, a handwritten note might seem more personal than voice mail.

How do you home in on the best choice for the difficult message you've got to deliver? "My overriding concern is:

How can I humanize this message?" says "power etiquette" speaker and author Dana May Casperson. "So when I owe an apology, I usually choose in-person first, a phone conversation as my top alternate, and a handwritten note next."

"My first choice is voice," says "The Telephone Doctor," Nancy Friedman, a consultant and trainer. "There's simply no match for the human voice, especially when we have something difficult or sensitive to say. Your voice has so much more than words: volume, tone, inflection, pitch, pauses, and so forth. You lose all of those with the written word."

But don't make the mistake of assuming that the more personalized approach is always the better choice for your difficult message. "E-mail can be the most caring and polite way to go," says Mary Mitchell, who heads Uncommon Courtesies, an etiquette and protocol consultancy. "For example, e-mail doesn't interrupt the recipient. It gives the recipient the chance to re-read and think before responding." That can be a plus in some cases, such as when the message you're delivering responds to a request you received from the recipient.

When one way won't do, take two.

Voice communication gives you a wide range of tonal signals that can ensure your attitude is conveyed as strongly as your language. Written communication means you've got a record, which can be critical in these litigious times. Why choose? Use both. You can often gain the unique advantages of both spoken and written words by delivering your message both ways—for example, a face-to-face visit or phone call, coupled with a confirming letter or memo.

In writing, take pains to say how you feel.

Because so many of the signals conveyed by voice are lost in writing, learn to write in a way that conveys exactly how you feel. And say it two or more different ways. Nancy Friedman created the term "e-tone" for the miscommunication that can so easily occur "when I write my e-mail with a particular tone of voice in mind and you read it with a totally different tone."

That's why Friedman claims it's almost impossible to overuse words that express feelings. "Use 'please' and 'thank you' often. Say 'I'm happy to report' or 'sorry to say' or 'pleased to tell you.' Give your readers every signal and clue you can think of to tell them how you feel." She even advises a direct, up-front statement to introduce important or delicate written messages: *"Please read this e-mail knowing how much I admire your work and wish to make it even better." "Please know from the outset how disappointed I am about last week's meeting."*

Don't shirk from face-to-face so you can lob written grenades.

Some otherwise courteous people take on a super-aggressive personality when they're behind the wheel of a car. Similarly, says Mitchell, some of us take refuge behind a computer screen or telephone "and assume we can say anything we want to anyone—things we'd never say face-to-face."

Friedman calls it "distance-induced bravery," noting that—particularly when we're agitated—we can be tempted to fire off an e-mail with language we wouldn't think of uttering if the recipient were right there with us. No matter how you're communicating, choose your words as if you're within arm's length of the recipient—and don't wish to get decked by a roundhouse right.

Never deliver any message impulsively.

The ancient admonition to count to 10 or take a deep breath before responding to any provocation is true in spades for difficult business communications. A rash outburst can haunt a career for years—and today's technologies provide whole new avenues for instant oblivion. "You just input a few well-chosen words and click on your e-mail program's 'reply' button," says Bill Roiter, president of Executive Performance Consultation.

"You've got to remember to stop and rethink," says Casperson. "Your credibility is always on the line, particularly in business situations. Communication is always visible and is always being assessed by others."

Consider anything in writing as public information.

During Washington's Iran-Contra investigation, Col. Oliver North was surprised to learn that the e-mail messages he thought he'd deleted could be recovered and made part of the record. You're well advised to think whether adverse consequences could follow if any sensitive message you commit to writing were to be read by anyone but your intended recipient. "Always ask, 'Who else could read this?'" says Casperson. "Faxes and e-mail messages are easily intercepted."

Review the who, why, and what of every e-mail message you write. Consultant Bill Roiter advises constant monitoring of e-mail compositions to guard against "ECK"—E-mail Career Killers. "You write a cute reply to a colleague's e-mail message, a 'quick thought' to the boss about an important project, or an off-color joke meant only for a sales buddy in Asia. It ends with the quip about the boss's bad breath broadcast to the whole department, or the quick thought being misinterpreted because you wrote it hastily, or the joke offending the secretary of the guy your buddy forwarded it to in France."

Roiter observes that ECKs "stem from e-mail's two greatest assets: ease and speed." Deck the ECK, he advises, by thinking about your words as you input them, remembering that your intentions—such as good-natured kidding—may not come through in writing, carefully proofreading every message you compose, and—*after* proofreading—looking again at the names of everyone listed in your "TO:" and "CC:" blocks to ensure you've written nothing that could spell trouble with any of them.

Don't touch that dial—until you've thought about voice mail.

An internal survey by Buckman Laboratories found that an average 86% of the company's employees at any one time are not at their desks and able to receive calls. That's typical of many companies, which makes it important—particularly when you're calling to deliver a difficult or important message—to decide how you'll handle voice mail before you place a call. Is this a message that can be left as a recording? The answer will be "no" if there's no emergency and you need more than a minute to deliver it; or if it's important to hear the recipient's immediate reaction (including stunned silence). If you get bumped into voice mail under these circumstances, request a return call or give an approximate time that you'll call again.

But when urgency or other circumstances make voice

mail your only alternative, "use a whole lot of tender tact," advises Nancy Friedman. She suggests an opening that gets right to the bottom line: *"I'm sorry to say I can't give you that day off next week."* *"I have to tell you I'm disappointed in your report on the tech project."* In such cases, use a tone of voice that you feel is loaded with regret and empathy, because the quality of many voice recorders isn't sufficient to fully capture the feelings you think you're conveying. Also be ready to offset bad news with something good or encouraging: *"I'm sure I could approve a day off anytime later this month."* *"Your visuals for the tech*

> **Don't make the mistake of assuming that the more personalized approach is always the better choice for your difficult message.**

project meeting are excellent." And be prepared to deliver all the essentials of your message quickly, so you aren't foiled by a short recording time. If the recording time allows, you can follow your main message with details or additional explanation.

Follow up to confirm and clarify.

If your difficult communication is delivered by any means other than an unhurried in-person or phone conversation, use one of these direct methods to follow up as promptly as possible. Ask the recipient if your message was received and whether he or she has any questions or reactions. You'll almost certainly get some good feedback, plus the opportunity to fine-tune or elaborate to make your feelings clearer. "I don't even trust a message as routine as rescheduling a meeting to voice mail or e-mail alone," says Dana May Casperson. "Glitches and garbling can too easily occur."

Finally, remember that no rules are hard and fast.

Although Casperson argues forcefully for using the most humanizing medium for your difficult communications, she acknowledges that no rule is inviolable. "Until I received a condolence e-mail from a friend that touched me deeply and was in no way offensive, I probably would have opposed sending that sort of message electronically."

Mary Mitchell notes that, in all human interactions, "there are always three choices: one that's entirely correct, one that's entirely incorrect, and one or more—some-where in between—that are appropriate." That presents you with at least some measure of choice in almost any situation. If you recognize you can choose, apply your common sense, and keep these guidelines in mind—you'll do right by yourself and your recipients.

For Further Reading

Business Etiquette and Professionalism by M. Kay Dupont (1998, Crisp Publications)

The Complete Idiot's Guide to Business Etiquette by Mary Mitchell (1999, Alpha Books)

Power Etiquette: What You Don't Know Can Kill Your Career by Dana Mary Casperson (1999, AMACOM)

Reprint C9911B

Don't Push That Send Button!

· · ·

Nick Morgan

In 1999, *Harvard Management Communication Letter* (*HMCL*) ran an article boldly setting forth what we called "The Ten Commandments of E-mail." The piece attracted a good deal of healthy commentary about the role of this new form of communication in corporate life. It's about time to look back and see which commandments still make sense and which need revision— and whether any new ones are necessary.

Several years later, we are all much more proficient in the use of e-mail. Generational reluctance to use e-mail has faded away; indeed, seniors comprised the fastest-growing user segment last year. And yet, some of our bad habits have persisted, and a few new problems have emerged since the original piece ran.

The most important problem in 1999 was the already overwhelming overload of information, which was exacerbated by the widespread adoption of e-mail. E-mail is what the experts call a nearly "frictionless" form of communication, which means it's easy to do—you don't have to go to a post office or even find a stamp. Just push a button, and you can blanket the world with your thoughts.

Today, that situation has become entrenched. Nearly every modern corporate citizen is now on e-mail and has to deal with a vast amount of associated junk. In addition to junk e-mail, we now have pop-up ads and other forms of online irritation that slow down the daily chore of separating the useful information from the trash.

How can we deal with this even more acute crisis? Douglas Neal, a research fellow at CSC Research Services, advocates taking an active stance in controlling your e-mail flow, particularly with regard to educating your colleagues to use e-mail wisely. He says, "The point is that you have to take actions, not just be passive. You have to reward those who do good and explain to those who are doing wrong that they have done so. Don't get mad, get it changed! Those who suffer quietly will continue to suffer!"

Neal recommends a two-step process for coping with your e-mail. First, he says, analyze the e-mail you receive, charting whether it's useful or not and how often you get both kinds. Then, tactfully tell those who regularly send you lots of low-utility e-mail to stop doing so. Neal points out that overload is in the eye of the recipient: some are overwhelmed by 10 e-mails a day, whereas others can easily handle 100. Take a week or so to chart your incoming e-mail. Then you can organize it with an eye toward addressing any problems that the analysis brings to light.

In the short run, *HMCL* still recommends performing daily "triage" on your e-mail inbox. Scan the entire list, eliminating all the junk mail first. Then group the remaining mail by action needed, just as you would a

> Even your deleted e-mails can be resurrected and read in courtrooms by lawyers who are not friends of yours.

real inbox on your desk. The efficiency experts tell us that you should handle paper only once in an office, deciding when you first look at it whether to discard it, keep it for filing, or place it on the "do list." You can manage your e-mail overload in the same way.

Beyond the overload issue, the commandments we

brought back from the digital mountain in 1999 identified some other times you might want to think twice about hitting "send." (We've rephrased some of them slightly for today's more sophisticated e-mail users.)

1. Use e-mail only when it's the most efficient channel for your need.

In 1999, we said, "What most people seem to forget is that it's e-*mail*. It's really a modern form of something your great-grandparents used: the letter. The modern incarnation is best for short, informal messages that need to be both written and read. Messages that don't fall into that category might be better handled in a different way."

This was very good advice then, and it remains good advice. In fact, we now have even more options in our grab bag of communication channels: instant messages, text messaging, chat rooms, and even pager code for the teenage crowd.

Each of these other channels is faster, more immediate, and—this is key—more perishable than e-mail. E-mail is forever, and therein lies the rub. When you need to commit something to print, use e-mail. In the business world, that list of needs should be confined to concrete requests, queries, and responses. In other words, the bare-bones daily details of work.

For gossip, back chat, networking, water cooler

exchanges, and all those other delightful aspects of business wheel-greasing, use the telephone or one of the other digital forms, where the record is less complete. Or even a face-to-face meeting! (More about this later.)

For messages with a greater feeling of permanence, or more punch, consider writing a real letter, on nice stationery, signed and dated by hand, and mailed through the post. You'd be surprised at how great a personal impact a traditional letter can have in this era of digital impermanence.

2. Never print your e-mail.

This commandment has not stood up as well over time. We were trying to bring about the paperless office and save trees. But because of the litigious nature of our society, you may well want to keep printed copies of e-mail you've sent as well as e-mail sent to you. Of course, as we've all learned, even e-mail that's been deleted can be recovered, but why take a chance? Print it and take a minute to lament the undeniable fact that the paperless office won't arrive any time soon.

Tony DiRomualdo, strategy and IT researcher, says, "We should not forget that e-mail is a very powerful and persistent medium that poses real and significant risks to companies. Surely the Andersen/Enron scandal holds many lessons about this point. And if used for the wrong purposes it can have nasty consequences. Don't say anything you would not want the entire planet to read at some point." But if you insist on saying something potentially actionable, keep a copy for your own records.

3. Send nothing over e-mail that must be error-free.

Time has only strengthened our opinion that this commandment is right on target. We said then, "It is simply impossible to proofread successfully on the computer screen." That is just as true now as it was then. If a communication must be error-free, then print it out, pick up something like an old-fashioned ruler, and read away, slowly, line by line. Then reread it backwards, word by word. And remember that spell checkers don't catch the wrong word spelled correctly. Get someone else to read your words, too.

4. Never delete names from your address book.

This advice remains especially pertinent for the virtually challenged. And yet it hardly seems like the biggest challenge we face today in the virtual world. It will save time to keep an up-to-date address book and to know how to use it. But not much time, unless you're prone to sending out a good many broadcast e-mails. And why would you want to do that? That usually comes under the heading of "spam," and it's at the heart of the problem of information overload.

5. Never forward chain e-mail.

Since 1999, there has been no lessening of this scourge! It is a practice universally decried, and yet we all know people who do it—and most of us will admit to having perpetrated a chain e-mail ourselves late on a Friday when everyone else has left early and we're still stuck in the office.

6. Never send e-mail when you're furious or exhausted.

This is even better advice than we knew at the time. Look at Microsoft, for example. The e-mails key players sent got them their day in court, and it wasn't what they wanted. It's an example we all can learn from. Legally, e-mail belongs to the company that provides the system and the link-up. You don't have privacy as an individual. And the court can wrest the e-mail records from the company, as happened to Microsoft. Don't—*don't*—commit anything to writing you wouldn't want to have read in court. Period.

7. Don't pass on rumor or innuendo about real people.

We repeat this advice in recalling the British man who boasted about his sexual exploits of the night before in an e-mail, only to see the boast spread out to thousands of e-mail recipients in a matter of hours. Avoid spreading false information about real, live people. It will come back to haunt you. Even your deleted e-mails can be resurrected and read in courtrooms by lawyers who are not friends of yours.

8. Nor should you do so about companies you work for or may work for one day.

In the intervening years, this practice has grown up and become a Web site. Most companies have at least one rogue site that mocks them, slanders them, or disses their products. Apparently, this advice pertains only to a distant, more civilized era—say, 1999. And these Web sites sure are handy when you're considering a job offer from a company that has one.

9. Never substitute e-mail for a necessary face-to-face meeting.

Anecdotal evidence of layoffs accomplished via e-mail only serves to reinforce this point. Here's what we said then, and every manager should have these sentences bronzed and placed in a conspicuous place in the office: "Never reprimand, reward, or fire someone who reports to you via e-mail. There's a special circle of hell awaiting those who do. We owe it to our humanity to perform these obligations, whether difficult or easy, in person. And remember that when you're trying to persuade someone to do something, or someone wants to persuade you, there is no substitute for a face-to-face meeting."

10. Remember this hierarchy: first the meeting, then the phone call, then the voice mail, then the e-mail.

This commandment still holds true: for the greatest impact, hold a meeting. You get more "bandwidth" face to face. The phone call eliminates the body language, but maintains tone and live exchange. Voice mail gets tone but does without live exchange. And an e-mail is neither live nor terribly nuanced. Hence the frequent misunderstandings about jokes attempted over e-mail, and those annoying but necessary little dingbats people use to signal emotion.

Final score: 80% of the Ten Commandments of E-mail still hold true. Some 20% have not held up or are now irrelevant. What about advice we would give now that we didn't then? Just one, our eleventh commandment:

11. Your e-mail is hackable and retrievable, and it can be used against you. Use only when absolutely necessary.

E-mail is an extremely efficient form of communication when used sensibly—but be careful out there. It's a litigator's paradise.

Reprint C0208E

Negotiating When Emotions Run High

. . .

As a manager, you engage in many workplace negotiations every day—whether you're forging a major business deal, trying to persuade your boss to approve a new program, or attempting to encourage a direct report to improve his or her performance. And during any negotiation, attention to etiquette becomes particularly crucial. Make a misstep, such as escalating emotional tension or aggressively holding your ground, and you risk losing your bargaining edge or, worse, watching your carefully crafted deal go south.

The articles in this section offer helpful advice for avoiding this scenario. Strategies include helping your negotiation counterpart save face during a tense round of bargaining, as well as managing that particularly delicate negotiation challenge: saying no to a boss's unreasonable request—and holding your ground when he or she protests.

You'll also find suggestions for using emotions strategically while bargaining. As one example, it's advantageous to create a warm, friendly atmosphere early in a negotiation—when you and your counterpart are most likely to explore creative options for mutually beneficial agreements. Expressing some anger (even if you don't feel it) later in a negotiation, when both parties move to claim value from the deal, can gain you further advantages.

When Life Gives You Lemons

How to Deal with Difficult People

• • •

Susan Hackley

Marty Spence was logging off his computer on Friday afternoon and eagerly looking forward to picking up his family to head to their lakeside home for the weekend. His boss suddenly appeared and said, "Marty, I need you to finish the Delcourt proposal so it's on their desks first thing Monday morning. I've got to catch a plane. No problem, right? I know I can count on you."

Spence quickly calculated that it would take most of the weekend to finish the proposal. Everyone else had already left, and his boss was headed for the door. The job would be dumped in his lap if he didn't say something fast. He was furious; this wasn't the first time his boss had asked him to take care of a problem he should have handled himself. What should he do?

As William Ury, author of *Getting Past No: Negotiating with Difficult People* (Bantam Books, 1991), explains, we all have to negotiate at times with difficult people. They might be stubborn, arrogant, hostile, greedy, or dishonest. Even ordinarily reasonable people can turn into opponents: A teenage daughter can be charming one moment and hurl insults at you the next. Your boss can be collaborative and understanding most of the time but make unreasonable demands on a Friday afternoon.

Holding Your Ground

Dealing with difficult people can be challenging, and doing it effectively calls for special skills.

In *Getting Past No,* Ury describes his five-step strategy for dealing with hard bargainers and difficult people. He calls his method "breakthrough negotiation," a way to "change the game from face-to-face confrontation into side-by-side problem-solving."

When his boss demanded his help, Marty Spence's first impulse could have been to strike back. "You've had three months to work on this proposal, and I've asked several times if you needed help. I'm not giving up my weekend plans to bail you out at the eleventh hour." If he chose this path, he would be standing up for himself but possibly jeopardizing his relationship with his boss. Alternatively, he could have caved in and said, "Sure, you can count on me." Then he would have had to face his

> Sometimes, even with joint problem solving, you need to convey a firm and clear "no." How do you say no while still preserving the relationship?

disappointed family and deal with his own anger at having been unfairly used.

Another option would have been to try to engage his boss in joint problem solving. "You've got a plane to catch, and I'm headed out the door to pick up my family. It's important that I be there on time. I'd like to help you. I wish I had known about this earlier. Let's see what ideas we can come up with." This response acknowledges the boss's predicament—he has a plane to catch—while establishing that Spence has his own commitment. It suggests that together they may be able to come up with a solution (e.g., bring in someone else to help, each cut their weekend short by a half day, submit an incomplete report, or tell the client the report will be delivered at the end of the day on Monday).

When You Need to Just Say No

Sometimes, even with joint problem solving, you need to convey a firm and clear "no." No, you won't work all weekend. No, your household budget cannot afford a new Jaguar. No, your assistant can't work from home two days a week. No, it's not acceptable that your supplier's delivery will be a month late. How do you say no while still preserving the relationship?

In his seminar *How to Say No . . . and Still Get to Yes,* offered by the Program on Negotiation at Harvard Law School, Ury suggests sandwiching the no between two "yeses." First, say yes to your own interests and needs. Then say no to the particular demand or behavior. Finally, say yes as you make a proposal.

In the case of the assistant wanting to work from home, you may learn about her interests and still decide that they aren't compelling enough for you to agree to her request. You first explain your *interest*: "I want to have our team here working together and sharing ideas. I value your contribution and need you to be part of that team." Then comes the *no*: "I understand your concerns about the long commute, but I've decided that you can't work from home two days a week." Finally, a *proposal*: "We can talk about having you work from home occasionally, and we can talk about arranging your hours differently so you avoid peak commuting hours. Or we can discuss reassigning you to a different job where it's not as important for you to be here physically."

Facing the Challenge

It can be extremely challenging to stand up to difficult people who may have an arsenal of weapons, including ridicule, bullying, insults, deception, and exaggeration. In some cases, they might attack you; in others, they might avoid confrontation. Sometimes you are taken by surprise; at other times, there might be a chronic problem you need to address.

For example, if your ex-husband regularly belittles you in front of your children, don't just trade insults. Find a time when you can have a real conversation without interruption. Let him know how his remarks make you feel. Encourage him to talk about why he says these things. Ask questions, and make him feel heard. Then discuss your shared interest in the children's happiness.

Whenever possible, prepare in advance for difficult negotiations. First of all, know yourself. What are your hot-button issues? What is essential to you? What is unacceptable? Next, think about what you are likely to hear from your opponent and plan how you might react.

Consider the following golf analogy. Jack Nicklaus says that every golfer should regularly take a lesson that focuses on basics such as grip and alignment, because if your setup is sound, there's a decent chance you'll hit a reasonably good shot. Similarly, every skilled negotiator should do a prenegotiation inventory. Ask yourself, What are my goals? What is my strategy? What is my walkaway point? Like the proper setup in golf, if you plan your negotiation with focused preparation, you improve your chances of ending up with a good outcome.

Build a Golden Bridge

Once you have brought your difficult opponent to the table, you may need to build a "golden bridge," Ury's term for letting your opponent save face and view the outcome as at least a partial victory. Even when your boss comes into your office on Friday afternoon with an inconsiderate request, you need to say no in a way that conveys your respect for him as your boss. And you want your assistant to feel that you appreciate her contributions, even if you can't agree to let her work at home. Finally, you want your ex-spouse to know that you value his parenting, even while you ask him to stop belittling you for the good of the children.

So how do you help your difficult opponent save face, while still standing up for yourself? Ury suggests reframing the problem so that you draw your opponents in the direction you want them to move. By way of example, he relates a story told by filmmaker Steven Spielberg, who was relentlessly bullied by an older boy when he was about 13 years old. Spielberg figured he couldn't beat the bully at his game, which was to use physical force, so he *changed the game,* inviting him to play a war hero in a movie he was making about fighting the Nazis. As Spielberg describes it, "I made him the squad leader in the film, with helmet, fatigues, and backpack. After that, he became my best friend."

This illustrates a key concept: involve your opponent in finding a solution. It's unlikely that a difficult person is going to accept your proposal fully, no matter how reasonable it is. Give him some choices: Would you prefer to meet at your office or mine? I could either pay a lump sum or make payments over time; which is better for you?

Hostage negotiators look for ways to build rapport and let the hostage takers save face, with the hope that the hostage takers will become more reasonable. The negotiators listen attentively to what the hostage takers want, whether it's an apology, a conversation with a loved one, a cup of coffee, or an acknowledgment of their grievance. The negotiators take careful notes, hoping to find something that will give them leverage.

Similarly, you should pay careful attention to your opponent, realizing that some of her needs may be unstated. A business owner who won't engage in problem solving to help close a deal to sell her business may turn out to have deep-seated ambivalence about selling. Realizing that, you might structure the deal as a joint venture, with a role for her in the new company.

Listen to Learn

If there is a common denominator in virtually all successful negotiations, it is to be an *active listener,* by which Ury means not only to hear what the other person is saying but also to listen to what is behind the words. Active listening is something frequently talked about but rarely done well; it is a subtle skill that requires constant, thoughtful effort. A good listener will disarm his oppo-

---

Breakthrough Negotiation

In *Getting Past No,* William Ury outlines five steps for negotiating with a difficult opponent, whether it's a boss, coworker, customer, salesclerk, or spouse.

1. **Don't react: Go to the balcony.** When someone is difficult, your natural reaction might be to get angry—or to give in. Instead, take yourself mentally to a place where you can look down objectively on the dispute and plan your response. Anytime you find your hot buttons getting pushed, try "going to the balcony."
2. **Disarm them by stepping to their side.** One of the most powerful steps to take—and one of the most difficult—is to try to understand the other person's point of view. Ask questions and show genuine curiosity.

nent by stepping to his side, asking open-ended questions, and encouraging him to tell you everything that is bothering him. Beyond that, Ury says, "he needs to know that you have heard [and understood] what he has said." So sum up your understanding of what he has said and repeat it in his own words.

Ury points out that there is a big payoff for you: "If you want him to acknowledge your point, acknowledge his first." And you may find you have little choice but to do this—how else to avoid a stalemate?

3. **Change the game: Don't reject—reframe.** You don't have to play along with a difficult person's game. Instead of locking into a battle of will or fixed positions, consider putting a new frame on the negotiation.
4. **Make it easy to say yes.** Build a golden bridge. Look for ways to help your opponent save face and feel that he's getting his way, at least in some matters. Using objective standards of fairness can help create a bridge between your interests.
5. **Make it hard to say no.** Bring them to their senses, not their knees. Use your power and influence to help educate your opponent about the situation. If she understands the consequences and your alternatives, she may be open to reason.

You Don't Have to Like Them

Dealing with difficult people does not mean liking them or even agreeing with them, but it does mean acknowledging that you understand their viewpoint.

Lakhdar Brahimi, a United Nations special envoy to Afghanistan in the aftermath of the September 11 terrorist attacks, was given the daunting task of negotiating with warlords and others who had caused many deaths, to try to create a stable government. He spoke of the need to negotiate with difficult people: "The nice people are sitting in Paris . . . To stop fighting, you've got to talk to the people who are doing the fighting, no matter how horrible they are . . . If I don't want to shake their hands, I shouldn't have accepted this job."

Whether you're negotiating with someone who is dangerously angry or only mildly annoying, the same skills are helpful in getting the results you want. Find out what your opponent wants and begin to build a case for why your solution meets her needs. If you're successful, you can turn your adversaries into your partners.

Reprint N0411C

Staying with No

* * *

Holly Weeks

Roger Fisher, negotiation expert and coauthor of the widely influential book *Getting to Yes,* used to tell his law students that sometimes he wished he had written a book about getting to no. He didn't have trouble saying no, he said, but he had trouble staying with the no: when family members were disappointed or associates pressed him, he would give up, and give in—even to things he didn't want to do.

Like Fisher, most of us want to be agreeable, we want to accommodate people. For one thing, people generally like us better when we say yes to them than when we say no. For another, saying no can be unpleasant—sometimes very much so. Particularly when we are saying no up—to someone senior—we feel considerable tension between our desire to stay with no and our desire to stay out of trouble.

The people to whom we say no rarely like hearing it, and it's no wonder. Our saying no signals rejection—of their ideas, of their wishes, of their priorities. Consequently, most people will try to get us to change the no to a yes. That means we have to work to defuse emotion on both sides: our discomfort at staying with an unpopular no and our counterpart's irritation, disappointment, or anger at hearing it.

We could, of course, cut the Gordian knot by giving in. But in the end, the consequences of not staying with no can cause much more damage—to your self-confidence, to your relationship with the other person, and to your credibility and effectiveness as a professional.

If we want to reduce the tension around staying with no, we will do better to think not about *whether* to stay with no, but *how*.

Many Reasons for the Other's Resistance

First, however, it helps to recognize why your counterparts want to "yes the no" and readjust your own emotional response to their efforts:

Business Culture

It isn't inherently insulting to you that the other person wants you to back off your no—it's part of our business climate to try to yes the no. If you want to keep the emotional temperature cool, don't read her challenging your no as an affront to your dignity or credibility.

Personal Experience and Expectations

Your counterpart's personal experience and expectations rather than the interpersonal relations between you may be the strongest determinant of how he responds to your no. He may be argumentative, wheedling, stunned, or angry because that's how he always handles hearing no.

I was staying with no in a conversation with a lawyer until I was eventually persuaded to his view. After I agreed, however, he kept right on hammering me to change my mind. Finally I laughed and said, "But Peter, I'm agreeing with you."

He paused and said, "Mostly people don't."

Context

There may be something about your staying with no—maybe something interpersonal, maybe not—that makes your no particularly difficult to accept. It's not unusual, for example, for someone who might be able to hear a no privately to be embarrassed to consent to it publicly. She may want you to back down so she can save face.

Not all of the friction between the effort to stay with no and the effort to yes the no is bad, but some of it is. Bad friction turns into a contest of wills, with one side winning and the other caving in or backing down. That's hard on relationships and often leads to payback.

Your Own Resistance

While your counterpart's resistance to your no can be hard to take, part of the problem may lie on your side, even if it doesn't feel that way. Far more people are coached to yes the no than to stay with no. Anyone who simply picks up a general interest magazine is instructed never to take no for an answer; in contrast, those of us who are trying to stay with no get very little guidance. So without practiced techniques to fall back on, we respond emotionally.

> Think of the push-pull between us as an honest disagreement about how the tension should be resolved.

Staying with no puts us in two different predicaments. On the one hand, we don't like to be negative. On the other, we don't like to be pushed. If you especially don't like to be negative, you probably tend to soften your no. It feels natural to you to try to stay with no gently. But this may result in your no not getting heard.

If you especially don't like to be pushed, you likely tend to become combative as you stay with no. For you, the natural thing is to get the conversation over with, not stretch it out. The problem with this strategy is that it may require you to spend a lot of time on after-the-fact damage control.

The solution in both cases is to change how you say no—that's the piece you can control. You need to acquire the skill of saying and staying with no neutrally—to say no simply, clearly, and directly, using arguments that are not easily weakened by your counterpart.

The Neutral No

A neutral no is steady, uninflected, and clear. It's mostly illustrated by what it's not. It's not harsh, it's not pugnacious or apologetic, it's not reluctant or heavily buffered, and it's not overly nice. Neutral and nice are not the same. Even if you're nice, use neutral to stay with no.

By sticking with neutral, you're concentrating on the business end of no, not the personal. If your first no is tentative, your second is brusque, and your third is caustic, I don't necessarily hear your intentions, whatever they may be. It's not my job to read intentions. I hear that first you give me hope and then you lose your temper. That's hard on relationships and on your reputation.

You want a referee's manner. A ref just says what he says—good news for some, bad news for others—regardless of the strong feelings on both sides that his message may inspire. His job is to give his message neutrally and stay with it neutrally if challenged.

A neutral manner doesn't prevent you from speaking directly about the friction between staying with no and trying to yes the no. "It's hard for me to tell you no; it must be hard for you to hear" is consistent with neutral. Use your own language here, but check that what you say is neutrally spoken:

- If you know or suspect why your counterpart is resisting your no, acknowledge his concern honestly but without giving hope. "You have a lot invested in what you're asking, and it looks like I'm personally blocking you." Give a reason or justification for your no. "I see my job as balancing valid, but competing, needs. I'm focusing on that." Aren't you just creating an opening for an argument there? Sometimes, yes. But the objective of staying with no is not necessarily to terminate this conversation with a monosyllable.

- If your reason is well chosen and neutrally spoken, stay with it. Don't volley different arguments with your counterpart. Changing an argument is not necessarily an improvement over repetition.

- In some cases, you may want to tell your counterpart what you could say yes to. That's not a foundation of staying with no, it's an option and the beginning of a negotiation. If you're open to that, you don't have to wait for the counterpart to ask.

Do's and Don'ts

Keep Your Eye on the Issue, Not the Personal

You see your job as staying with no; I see my job as yessing that no. No one is doing anything wrong—we just don't want the same outcome here. It helps to think of the push-pull between us as an honest disagreement about how the tension should be resolved. It does not help to think of my resistance to your no as disrespect for you.

Know Your Triggers

Your counterpart may be trying out different tactics to get you to yes your no. The tactic the counterpart uses matters only if you're vulnerable to it. Which arguments are you most susceptible to? Which tactics? Does an ominous suggestion that the union will hear about this roll off or rattle you? Do tears move you to offer a tissue or to fold? Most of us know where we're vulnerable. If, for example, you are undermined by a counterpart who says she is disappointed in you and personally let down because you stay with no, you have probably been vulnerable to that sense of falling short of expectations before.

Don't Give Them Too Much to Read

It is very hard to pick out what part of a message to read if, first, the message is mixed and, second, there's an emotional flare in it. A harsh no that offends or angers people makes them stick to their guns, even if all you wanted to do was get the conversation over with. On the other hand, people who are uncomfortable staying with no often overdo the apologetic nature of their no—they say no, express their regret for it, and ask to be forgiven for staying with no, all at the same time. The message surrounding the no seems to be, "I want to stay with no and yet have you like me." That's hard to read, but more important, if I don't want to hear the no, it's very easy for me to overlook it.

Don't Weaken Your No

Curiously, many people do this backward. They start saying no using lightweight reasons, holding back the real, heavyweight reason. And the counterpart swats away the little reasons because they aren't very persuasive. To limit the frustration on both sides, give reasons with good weight up front.

An executive assistant had been helping out a colleague by taking on work that was not his responsibility. Now he needed to curtail his tendency to say yes all the time because he was swamped. The next time his colleague asked for his customary help with photocopying, he said, "I have to say no, and it's really my fault because I don't seem to be managing my time very well." His colleague disagreed that he wasn't managing his time well—in fact, she praised how well he managed his time. And, not accepting that the executive assistant had a time-management fault, the colleague also didn't accept his no.

He had offered a self-criticism with his no because he wanted to head off the potential criticism that he wasn't being very helpful. But he weakened his no by doing so.

Beware Misguided Empathy

Most of us genuinely regret it if our counterpart is disappointed when we stay with no. But be careful and clear about what you can legitimately claim to share.

A newly married couple was surprised and upset to have their mortgage application declined by their new bank. The mortgage officer agreed that it was disappointing. She listened to their protests and arguments, making suggestions while staying with no. But as the couple was leaving her office, she said, "Believe me, I feel as bad about this as you do." The young wife turned to her, stiff with new indignation, and said, "No. You don't."

The mortgage officer undermined her good no by claiming that her pain was as great as theirs. That will almost never feel right to those who must accept the no.

Avoid a Battlefront Attitude: "I Won't Give In; You Lose"

Not everyone tries to soften her no. Some of us say no combatively, and treat staying with no as escalating warfare. This could be you if you find a battle of wills stimulating. When staying with no feels like a triumph of the will, good outcomes—and good judgment—are in jeopardy.

Don't Give False Hope

Staying with no tentatively, or with a show of reluctance, makes it easy for your counterpart to hope you will change your no—and hard for him to accept the no. It sounds like your no is on the edge of tipping over into yes, so your counterpart is encouraged to keep pushing. Try the positive approaches suggested here to break a pattern of giving in, instead of falling back on a manner of saying no that suggests you are about to give in.

Practice Staying with No; Don't Avoid It

If you want to get better at staying with no in the face of the arguments and tactics that trigger you, it makes sense to practice with someone who will play the part of your worst nightmare in a protected setting. That's better than waiting until a real situation arises, when a lot is on the line.

You want to practice for four reasons: (1) so you'll stay with your message, (2) so you won't edit it on your feet, (3) so you'll know what it's going to feel like to say it, and (4) so you can see whether you really want to stay with this no—or whether you should yes it.

Reprint C0410A

Great Expectations

. . .

Max H. Bazerman

How often have you heard a friend or colleague refer to a contract as being "in the bag," only to find out later that the deal didn't go through? There always turns out to be a good reason a negotiation fell apart. Yet the fact remains that most negotiators are overconfident about their chances of reaching agreement. And when they're haggling over money, negotiators routinely overestimate their ability to get opponents to agree to a desired price.

A common cognitive bias, *overconfidence* causes us to have unrealistically high expectations of success, in negotiation and in many other aspects of life. Psychologists Amos Tversky and Daniel Kahneman explain overconfidence in terms of *anchoring*. When assessing a situation, we start with what we believe to be true (in negotiation, what we believe the other side will find acceptable) and inadequately adjust away from that anchor, overlooking the full range of possible outcomes. The failure to adjust from a biased anchor leads us to the false belief that our original estimate will be right on target.

In past columns, we've explored various biases that affect negotiation. Why are sloppy cognitive shortcuts so hard to shake? One reason is overconfidence. The effects of many biases can snowball, making your confidence in your judgments increasingly irrational. Notably, overconfidence is most likely to flare up regarding moderate or difficult issues—bad news for managers facing complex, high-stakes negotiations.

Think you may be immune to overconfidence? Test yourself with this little quiz.

Listed below are 10 uncertain quantities, adapted from recent items in *Harper's Magazine*'s Index. On a separate sheet of paper, jot down your best estimate of the quantity for each item. Next, put a lower and upper bound around your estimate, such that you're 98% confident that your range surrounds the actual quantity.

Do not look up any information on these items or look ahead in the article.

  a. As of 2003, amount of annual worldwide governmental fishing subsidies.

  b. As of 2001, the number of U.S. children under age 18 who become regular cigarette smokers every day.

c. The 2002 GDP of Liberia.

d. Rank of Belgium's water quality among 122 countries assessed by the United Nations.

e. Estimated cost of vaccinating the 745,000 children who died worldwide from measles in 2001, according to the World Health Organization.

f. Average 2002 salary of a U.S. state legislator.

g. Average amount spent lobbying a U.S. state legislator in 2002.

h. As of 2000, the total amount of money the U.S. Defense Department has lost track of, according to a report by its inspector general.

i. Amount of money owed the U.S. government by securities-law violators between 1995 and 2001.

j. Rank of Hungary among nations whose residents are most likely to be obese.

How many of your 10 ranges will actually surround the true quantities? See the box at the end of the chapter for the answers. If you set your ranges so that you were 98% confident, you should expect to correctly capture approximately 9.8, or 9 to 10, of the quantities.

How did you do? If your ranges surrounded 9 or 10 of the correct quantities, then you were appropriately confident in your estimation ability. If you're like most people, you surrounded between three (30%) and seven (70%) of the quantities, despite being 98% confident. In other words, if you're like most people, you didn't do so well.

> We're likely to be overconfident in estimating both the position of a neutral third party and the likelihood that the third party will accept our point of view.

You might be thinking that this quiz was unfair—after all, who keeps up on global fishing subsidies or Belgium's water supply? That's exactly the point. When you're unsure about something, admit it! Those who perform well on the quiz recognize their uncertainty. Sensing that their guesses are way off, they hedge their bets by surrounding the estimates with an extremely broad range.

Overconfidence is a fundamental human bias and is hardly limited to expectations of high achievement in trivia quizzes. It is especially common in the workplace; it's been observed among members of the armed forces, CIA agents, CEOs, audit partners, negotiators, and in people working in numerous other professions on whom we rely for accurate information.

Overconfidence on the Job

You might be asking yourself if overconfidence is necessarily a bad thing. After all, it has probably given you the courage to take important risks, stretch your abilities, and thrive in many arenas. Unwarranted confidence can indeed be beneficial in some circumstances. But consider the potential adverse effects of excess confidence in the following workplace dilemmas:

1. You are the chief legal counsel for a firm that has been threatened with a multimillion-dollar lawsuit. You feel 90% confident that the firm will not lose in court. Is this degree of certainty sufficient for you to recommend rejecting an out-of-court settlement?

Now suppose you learn that if you lose the case, your firm will go bankrupt. Based on this new information, are you still comfortable with your 90% estimate?

2. Your company has been the main supplier of a critical part to an automobile manufacturer. In recent years, your contract with the buyer has averaged $300 million

annually. This year, the automaker put the contract up for auction, and seven other companies submitted bids. Certain that your product is the best in the industry, you slightly increased your price from last year.

You're 80% confident that you'll be the winning bidder—but if you lose, your company will have to close a plant and lay off 1,500 employees. Are you still optimistic about your ability to bring home the contract?

These examples demonstrate the serious problems—bankruptcy, layoffs, loss of personal credibility—that can result from the tendency to be overconfident. While confidence in your abilities is necessary for achievement in life, overconfidence can be a barrier to effective professional decision making.

> When overconfidence gets in the way of rational throught and analysis, it can have devastating consequences.

Major league baseball offers a graphic example of overconfidence in action. When a baseball team and a player disagree about compensation, a system exists that calls for the player and owner to submit final offers to an arbitrator. In *final-offer arbitration,* the arbitrator is required to weigh the offers and accept one position or the other; compromise is not allowed. For both owner and player, the goal is to come slightly closer than the opposition to the arbitrator's perception of the appropriate compensation package.

Margaret Neale and I asked negotiators in a simulated final-offer arbitration to estimate the probability that an arbitrator would accept their offer. Because the arbitrator had to accept one of two offers in its entirety, the overall probability that a particular offer would be accepted was 50%. On average, negotiators estimated that their final offers had a 68% chance of being chosen by the arbitrator. They believed their offers were 18% more likely to be accepted than could actually be true. We're likely to be overconfident in estimating both the position of a neutral third party and the likelihood that the third party will accept our point of view.

Such overconfidence diminishes incentives to compromise. After all, if you're sure you'll win, why give anything away? The failure to make wise tradeoffs often leads to disappointment at the bargaining table.

Curb Your Overconfidence

Objectivity is the key to reducing overconfidence. In arbitration, for example, the more objective your assessment of the opponent's offer and the position of the arbitrator, the better equipped you'll be to use this information strategically.

How can you improve your objectivity? First, some good news: simple training about the existence of overconfidence goes a long way toward reducing bias. In a research study, Margaret Neale and I trained one group of negotiators about the hazards of overconfidence. We gave another group of negotiators no training at all. All negotiators then engaged in a final-offer arbitration simulation. Relative to the trained negotiators, the untrained negotiators were unreasonably confident in their judgments and were significantly less likely to compromise and reach agreement prior to arbitration.

The implication? Simply by reading this column, you may have already reduced your tendency to be overconfident. But the bias is deeply ingrained, and this is only a small first step. Here are some other ways to improve your negotiation performance.

Embrace Uncertainty

As your objectivity increases, so will your uncertainty about your probability of success. Smart negotiators accept uncertainty as an integral part of decision making. By acknowledging your own uncertainty about the future and about the other side's position, you'll become more willing to propose and accept the type of compromises that lead to mutually beneficial agreements.

Enlist a Third Party

In third-party mediation, feuding parties hire professional mediators to help them reach a voluntary agreement. Mediators often focus on reducing negotiators' confidence in the "correctness" of their positions. This strategy is useful outside of formal third-party contexts as well.

When you're preparing for an important negotiation, seek out an objective critique of your plans from a disinterested adviser. You can hire a professional consultant, speak off the record with a colleague at another firm, or seek help from a friend whom you trust to be blunt and honest with you. Whether you're paying the third party for his advice or not, it's essential that he has no stake in your success. Few negotiators bother to reach out to an adviser. Those who do are sure to gain an edge.

Itemize Your Errors

When an adviser is not available or appropriate, as in many negotiations between buyers and sellers, there are other ways to reduce your overconfidence. One strategy that has proven successful in research studies involves asking people to explain why their judgments might be wrong, or at least considerably off the mark. Calling individuals' attention to obvious errors can lead them to clearer thinking about the negotiation ahead.

You can try this strategy yourself. Before any negotia-

The Answers

a.	$15 billion	f.	$30,300
b.	3,000	g.	$130,000
c.	$560 million	h.	$1.1 trillion
d.	122	i.	$3.1 billion
e.	$558,750	j.	3

tion, seek out data that could lead you to revise your plans. Research the other party's position, as well as people who have been in your shoes in the recent past. Don't just look on the bright side—account for potential strikes against you as well. By facing up to your bargaining weaknesses, you'll increase your odds of proposing an offer that's acceptable to the other side. Once talks are under way, it will be much harder to update overconfident beliefs.

In some contexts, overconfidence is a valuable asset, motivating us to make beneficial changes in our lives and persevere in difficult situations. But when overconfidence gets in the way of rational thought and analysis, it can have devastating consequences. By guarding against overconfidence, you'll achieve a healthy and helpful self-confidence in your negotiating abilities.

Reprint N0401D

Emotional Strategy

. . .

Margaret A. Neale

We've all been in negotiations where we said or did something in the heat of the moment that later came back to haunt us. Maybe we shared information we shouldn't have or escalated commitment to a course of action that, in hindsight, was not in our best interest.

When emotions spiral out of control, our ability to think and act strategically is compromised. In his book *The Art and Science of Negotiation: How to Resolve Conflicts and Get the Best Out of Bargaining,* Howard Raiffa stresses the importance of self-control at the bargaining table, especially when it comes to our emotions and their visibility.

There is undeniable wisdom in this advice. But it's not always the case that strong emotions work against us or that suppressing emotion is the best course of action. In fact, as I will explain, emotion can work to your advantage by providing information about your counterpart's priorities, sharpening your decision-making skills, enhancing your ability to claim value, and encouraging collaborative value creation.

The Right Way to Regulate Emotion

Emotional flooding—when strong, specific, and often negative feelings overwhelm us—poses obvious hazards to negotiators, who need to be able to think clearly when faced with the complex, strategically demanding task of creating and claiming value. For this reason, emotional regulation can be an essential component of negotiation. But different types of regulation create different results.

In a 2000 study, James Gross, Jane Richards, and Oliver John explored the social and cognitive costs of two forms of emotional regulation: *suppression,* or controlling one's emotions by not expressing them; and *reappraisal,* or controlling emotions by changing the way one thinks about the situation.

When your counterpart makes a personal attack against you, you might suppress your emotions in an attempt to resist "rising to the bait." But if you expect your opponent to try to put you off balance at key moments, you can use the attack to help you identify important issues.

Comparing the effect of these two regulation strategies, the researchers found that negotiators who suppressed their emotion experienced impaired cognitive processing. What's more, they were less well liked by their counterparts, a fact that may have diminished their ability to engage in future joint value creation.

It's unwise to suppress emotions in negotiations, and not just because suppression is likely to lead to worse outcomes and greater rancor. Trying to suppress a feeling that comes on strong—such as the outrage you may feel after being issued a threat—can be almost impossible. Emotions provide both you and your counterpart with unique information that may lead to mutually beneficial outcomes.

> It's not always the case that strong emotions work against us or that suppressing emotion is the best course of action.

Instead of trying to suppress your feelings, consider when you may be subject to strong emotional experiences in advance and reappraise the situation *before* experiencing the emotion. Through reappraisal, you can focus on the meaning of a situation and anticipate your emotional reaction. What if you decided ahead of time to view a threat as providing important information about what the other side values? Rather than reacting emotionally, you could use the information to adjust aspects of future proposals.

Anger: The Good and the Bad

Most negotiations are "mixed motive" in structure, requiring us both to compete to claim value and to cooperate to create value. The ability to move back and forth between these two goals is a critical—and difficult—skill.

How do emotions affect value creation and claiming? Researchers Alice Isen and Peter Carnevale found that a positive mood leads to greater value creation. Good feelings may signal that a situation is low in risk. With little need for the vigilance associated with negative emotions, negotiators may be more willing to think creatively. By contrast, researchers historically have found that anger is more likely to be associated with value claiming.

But anger can actually hinder this process. In a 1997 study, Keith Allred, John Mallozzi, Fusako Matsui, and Christopher Raia found more complex results regarding the effects of anger and compassion on negotiation processes and outcomes. They compared negotiators who reported high levels of anger and low levels of compassion for each other with negotiators who had a more positive emotional regard for the other side. The "angry" negotiators achieved fewer joint gains and had less desire to work with each other in the future than did the more positively inclined group.

Surprisingly, angry negotiators did not claim any more value for themselves than the other negotiators. Angry

> Any emotion that triggers uncertainty can push a negotiator to do the cognitive work necessary to create value.

negotiators appear to incur costs from their negative emotions without any benefits.

What happens when anger is not focused on an individual? Nicholas Anderson of Stanford University and I conducted a study in which we provoked anger in one member of a pair of negotiators. Half of the angry negotiators were sure that their counterparts had attempted to provoke their anger, while the other half were unsure.

We found that this uncertainty led to *better* joint outcomes for angry negotiators. In fact, angry but uncertain negotiators created more value than emotionally neutral or slightly positively inclined negotiators, who, in turn, did better than angry but certain negotiators. Moreover, angry negotiators, in general, were able to claim a larger percentage of a resource than their counterparts were.

Subsequent analyses indicated that, while anger typically results in poor information processing, uncertainty about the source of one's anger could motivate the angry negotiator to engage in effective information processing.

The lesson here for negotiators is that focused anger stands in the way of value creation. But note that it's focus, not anger, that reduces the incentive to process information. Any emotion that triggers or is associated with uncertainty can inspire a negotiator to do the cognitive work necessary to create value. With anger comes the additional benefit of enhanced value claiming. Thus, an unpleasant phone conversation just before you walk into a negotiation may improve your outcomes—especially if the phone call and the negotiation are unrelated.

Catch the Feeling

Most of the existing research on affect in negotiation has focused on emotional experience rather than on emotional expression. Yet studies have shown that emotional expression can occur independently from feelings, making expression worthy of investigation.

Marwan Sinaceur and Larissa Tiedens of Stanford University recently found that negotiators made more concessions when facing counterparts who expressed (but did not necessarily feel) anger. Not only did those who expressed anger benefit by claiming more value, but they also did not lose their ability to create value. While experienced emotions may direct the way in which you process information, emotional expressions seem to in-

Emotion and Judgment

The work of University of Iowa neuroscientists Antoine Bechara, Daniel Tranel, and Hanna Damasio demonstrates the effect of emotion on decision making.

They study patients with ventromedial (VM) prefrontal cortex lesions. Individuals with such lesions have dramatically diminished emotional responses. Although their intellectual functioning and memory are unaffected, VM patients exhibit impaired decision-making ability. For example, one of their patients, "Elliot," would spend 30 minutes trying to choose between two possible dates for an appointment, using relatively sophisticated cost-benefit strategies that far exceeded the demands of the task.

In one experiment, Bechara and colleagues exposed both normal and VM patients to a gambling task. Participants were asked to choose one card at a time from among four decks. Every time a participant chose a card from the A or B deck, he won $100. Every time he picked a card from the C or D deck, he won $50.

But sometimes after drawing a card and receiving either $100 or $50, the participant was told that he had

fluence your counterpart's social inferences and subsequent behavior.

Expressing positive emotions may increase the willingness of your counterpart to agree to your proposals and to view you and the situation in a better light. While putting your counterpart in a good mood is a useful

to return a certain amount of his winnings. For the A and B decks, the unpredictable losses per 10 cards averaged $1,250; for the C and D decks, the unpredictable losses per 10 cards averaged $250.

In other words, choosing cards from the C and D decks resulted in the greatest net gains.

Normal subjects learned to pick from the C and D decks. But VM subjects preferred the A and B decks, which resulted in greater immediate gains but lower net gains. Moreover, as normal subjects gained experience in the task, they displayed physical signs of tension before the selection of a card; the VM subjects showed no such changes. In fact, the VM subjects continued to choose disadvantageously even *after* realizing the consequences of their actions.

Subjects lacking in emotion made bad decisions even when they knew what the right decision was.

The lesson? Low or moderate levels of emotion can prepare us for challenges and opportunities by providing us with information about our goals and our progress toward them.

strategy, it often can seem like an impossible goal. In fact, people transmit feelings to each other subconsciously, mimicking each other's facial expressions, body language, and speech patterns. If you smile, it's likely your counterpart will, too, which in turn may incline him to become happier.

Fritz Strack, Leonard Martin, and Sabine Stepper found that people rated cartoons as funnier when they were holding a pen in their teeth—using the muscles associated with smiling—than when holding a pen with their lips—using muscles incompatible with smiling. Merely mimicking a smile may trigger some of the benefits of smiling.

What this means is that negotiators may find it a smart strategy to express emotions that they do not necessarily experience. For instance, it can make sense to be especially warm and friendly early in the negotiation, so as to catalyze positive emotions in your counterpart at this stage, when value creating is most likely to occur. In later stages of the process, you might choose to express more negative emotions, such as anger, in an attempt to claim additional value for yourself.

We would all be worse off without the information gleaned from our emotional response to a negotiation. While feelings too often draw our attention away from the demands of an interaction, they can also serve as useful tools for interpreting and guiding your reactions and those of the other side.

Reprint N0502D

Putting On the Pressure

How to Make Threats in Negotiations

• • •

Adam D. Galinsky and Katie A. Liljenquist

On August 3, 1981, 12,000 air-traffic controllers went on strike after negotiations with the federal government about wages, hours, and benefits broke down. Then-president Ronald Reagan took an uncompromising stand: "It is for this reason that I must tell those who fail to report for duty this morning they are in violation of the law, and if they do not report for work within 48 hours, they have forfeited their jobs and will be terminated."

On August 5, true to his word, Reagan carried out his threat and fired the 11,359 air-traffic controllers who had not returned to work. Many observers view Reagan's controversial threat and follow-through as a pivotal moment in his presidency and the foundation for future political victories.

This story highlights the important role of threats in negotiations. Broadly speaking, a threat is a proposition that issues demands and warns of the costs of noncompliance. Even if neither party resorts to them, potential threats shadow most negotiations.

Threats can be invaluable in helping you achieve your interests. Researchers have found that people actually evaluate their counterparts more favorably when they combine promises with threats rather than extend promises alone. Whereas promises encourage exploitation, the threat of punishment motivates cooperation. But because threats can backfire in unintended ways, a skilled negotiator must learn to use them judiciously.

Recognizing that there is a time and place for threats, we open by detailing when to use them effectively, then present the *WISE* approach to threats: one characterized by willingness, interests, saving face, and exactness.

When to Make a Threat

Professor Jeanne Brett of Northwestern University and her colleagues have identified three situations in which threats can be a necessary and effective tactic. First, as negotiators attempt to push past a heated deadlock, threats might be required to get the other party to come to the bargaining table. Threatening aggression is one way to get representatives of an obstinate country, for example, to attend peace talks. Second, threats can be a weapon against recalcitrance, steering a negotiation from

> People actually evaluate their counterparts more favorably when they combine promises with threats rather than extend promises alone.

impasse toward settlement. A threat might be the only way to signal to bullies that they're not the only ones with muscle to flex. Finally, well-crafted threats may ensure that an agreement will survive the negotiation and secure implementation as well as follow-through.

Although threats serve a purpose, they can carry heavy consequences. A threat might provoke resistance. When people feel that their freedom is restricted, they react against a perceived loss of choice. For instance, researchers have found that individuals take longer to leave a parking space when another car is waiting for it than when no car is in sight. Similarly, by making a threat, you might actually *decrease* the probability that the other side will grant your wishes. Furthermore, an agreement made through coercion could be seen as illegitimate, leading the other side to violate its terms unless you apply additional threats. Imposing your threat could also incite a desire for vengeance. Psychologists have found that revenge has biological foundations, persisting until it is satisfied, like hunger. The more severe a threat's consequences, the more extreme the retaliation is likely to be.

Consequently, an effective threat satisfies your interests without creating such ill will that the agreement incurs vengeance. Your goal should be to make threats that invite the other side to both respect you and like you. Respect encourages credibility and compliance, while liking discourages defensiveness and defiance.

How to Make a WISE Threat

How can you make a threat that secures a positive outcome and cultivates both liking and respect? By making sure it's a WISE threat.

WISE Threats Express Willingness

When making a WISE threat, you must be willing to impose the stated consequences in the event of noncompliance, yet also make your demands sufficiently reasonable so the other side will be willing and able to comply with them. Once you've built up a sufficient cache of credibility, the mere possibility of a threat can be enough to rouse others to follow your desired course of action. By carrying out his threat to fire the striking air-traffic controllers, Reagan signaled to both Congress and the Soviet Union that he was not to be trifled with, making concessions from them easier to garner.

Demands must fall within the realm of what is feasible for the other side. As the late political scientist Karl Deutsch pointed out, "Even the most intense and credible threats may not stop people from sneezing." Don't make demands that your counterpart would be incapable of satisfying even if she wanted to.

WISE Threats Satisfy Interests

A WISE threat satisfies your own interests and targets the other side's interests. Consider whether the threat will truly help you achieve your broader goals. Issuing a threat might provide gratification, but it can also lock you into a particular course of action. In addition, carrying out a threat can be costly. To assess whether a threat will satisfy or violate your interests, answer the following three questions:

1. Is your threat based on emotion? Effective negotiators must be rational—immune to momentary pressures and volatile emotions.

And a threat should never be made under the influence of anger: multiple studies have linked anger to reduced information processing, risky behaviors, and clouded judgment. A reliable rule of thumb is never to make a threat that you did not plan in advance. This rule forces you to consider both the short-term and long-term consequences in a setting in which you are not captive to your emotions.

2. Will your threat incite a counterthreat that dwarfs your own? Driven by reaction and revenge, threats often provoke counterthreats. Before making a threat, assess the potential impact of a retaliatory response, lest you initiate a battle that you aren't prepared to fight.

3. Will the threat cost you more than it will cost the other side? Threats are not about punishing the opposition; they are about fulfilling your own interests. When you forget this important point, your desire to teach the other side a lesson may cause you to escalate a threat without regard to the toll it could take on you.

If you've determined that a threat would indeed serve your interests, make sure the threat will function as a motivator, not a punishment. Frame it in terms of how compliance will further your counterpart's interests rather than how noncompliance will thwart them.

Imagine a dispute between a handheld computer company, Jansen, and a community hospital, Riverside. Jansen wanted to become a leading player in the lucrative health-care market. At the same time, Riverside needed handheld computers to increase efficiency and improve

> The goal is to achieve implementation without resistance, compliance without vengeance, and respect without contempt.

its precarious financial situation. Jansen and Riverside agreed on an information management system but, once it was installed, they argued about whether customized software was included in the deal. Without the specialized software, Riverside might be forced into bankruptcy and Jansen probably would not be paid.

Riverside faced a choice. It could threaten to secure the software in the language of punishment: "If we can't reach agreement, you'll see little of your money." Alternatively, it could frame the threat in terms of Jansen's broader interests: "If we are forced into bankruptcy, you're unlikely to make progress in this attractive market.

However, if we can reach an agreement, you will be seen as our savior and could become a market leader." By centering the threat on the benefits of compliance, Riverside increased the probability of reaching an integrative agreement.

WISE Threats Save Face

A WISE threat allows you to save face—to survive the negotiation with pride intact. How will your threat affect the way the other party views you? How will it affect your long-term reputation? To be taken seriously in a negotiation, make sure the consequences are meaningful to the other side. If Reagan had merely threatened to revoke vacation days from noncompliant strikers, his warning most likely would have been dismissed.

Strikes and Consequences

In 1984, members of the Canadian Auto Workers Union went on strike against General Motors. Just as the workers predicted, when the assembly line ground to a halt, each day of the strike cost the company millions of dollars in lost production. After only 13 days, General Motors acquiesced to the union's principal demands.

The following year, Hormel meatpackers went on strike. In this case, management was prepared to keep

WISE threats also allow the other side to save face. Give the other side an easy way to meet your demands by providing alternatives that are of equal value to you. By permitting him to select the most palatable option, you let him comply without sacrificing his self-respect. Frame your threat so that he feels his compliance is a gift rather than a forced concession. Accordingly, when he meets your demands, you should respond with gratitude rather than smugness. By ensuring that both parties save face, you increase the chances that you will be both respected and liked.

WISE Threats Are Exact

WISE threats express unambiguous contingencies. When issuing a threat, lay out a causal "if, then" sequence of

production going, first by manning the factory themselves and then by hiring replacement workers willing to work for significantly less than the striking workers. Few of the striking workers' demands were ever met, and most lost their jobs permanently.

The same threat was issued in both instances, but the Hormel employees overestimated the impact of their warning, failing to realize that management had recourse to alternative labor. Ultimately, they became victims of their own actions.

events that attaches specific consequences to the other side's failure to meet your demands. By being precise in your demands, you increase the chance that the other side will fulfill your expectations. You should also offer a clear timeline and an escape route for avoiding the consequences of your threat.

To do so, you must know ahead of time what you want and when you want it. For example, you might state, "If we don't receive the required documentation from you by the end of the month, we will have to terminate services and pursue our legal rights. But if you meet our deadline, we will proceed as originally contracted." By being exact, you avoid future disputes about whether or not your demands were met.

"I consider it a mark of great prudence in a man to abstain from threats or any contemptuous expressions," Machiavelli once said. Given their potentially volatile yet expedient nature, threats must be issued with great care and thought. The goal is to achieve implementation without resistance, compliance without vengeance, and respect without contempt. Through the judicious use of WISE threats, you can reach agreements with both a handshake and a smile.

Reprint N0412B

About the Contributors

Stever Robbins is president of VentureCoach.com, an entrepreneurial coaching service.

Ken O'Quinn is a writing coach who conducts corporate seminars. He spent 22 years in journalism, mostly with the Associated Press, before starting his business, Writing with Clarity.

Monci J. Williams is a contributor to *Harvard Management Update*.

Constantine von Hoffman is a contributor to *Harvard Management Update*.

Nick Morgan is a contributor to *Harvard Management Update*.

Paul Michelman is a contributor to *Harvard Management Update*.

Lauren Keller Johnson is a contributor to *Harvard Management Update*.

Eric McNulty is a contributor to *Harvard Management Update*.

David Stauffer is a contributor to *Harvard Management Update*.

Susan Hackley is managing director of the Program on Negotiation at Harvard Law School. She was formerly a political and communications professional and cofounder of an Internet company.

Holly Weeks is a communications consultant.

About the Contributors

Max H. Bazerman is the Jesse Isador Straus Professor at the Harvard Business School and the vice-chair for research of the Program on Negotiation. He is author with Michael Watkins of *Predictable Surprises* (HBS Press, 2004).

Margaret A. Neale is the John G. McCoy–Banc One Corporation Professor of Organizations and Dispute Resolution at the Graduate School of Business at Stanford University and also is the faculty director for four executive education programs at Stanford.

Adam D. Galinsky is an associate professor at Northwestern University's Kellogg School of Management. His research interests include how particular strategies affect objective and subjective outcomes in negotiations, power, and influence of stereotypes and stigma on negotiations.

Katie A. Liljenquist teaches negotiation at the Kellogg School. Her research examines justifications of bad behavior and ethical pitfalls in negotiations.

Harvard Business Review Paperback Series

The Harvard Business Review Paperback Series offers the best thinking on cutting-edge management ideas from the world's leading thinkers, researchers, and managers. Designed for leaders who believe in the power of ideas to change business, these books will be useful to managers at all levels of experience, but especially senior executives and general managers. In addition, this series is widely used in training and executive development programs.

These books are priced at US$19.95
Price subject to change.

Title	Product #
Harvard Business Review **Interviews with CEOs**	3294
Harvard Business Review on **Advances in Strategy**	8032
Harvard Business Review on **Appraising Employee Performance**	7685
Harvard Business Review on **Becoming a High Performance Manager**	1296
Harvard Business Review on **Brand Management**	1445
Harvard Business Review on **Breakthrough Leadership**	8059
Harvard Business Review on **Breakthrough Thinking**	181X
Harvard Business Review on **Building Personal and Organizational Resilience**	2721
Harvard Business Review on **Business and the Environment**	2336
Harvard Business Review on **The Business Value of IT**	9121
Harvard Business Review on **Change**	8842
Harvard Business Review on **Compensation**	701X
Harvard Business Review on **Corporate Ethics**	273X
Harvard Business Review on **Corporate Governance**	2379
Harvard Business Review on **Corporate Responsibility**	2748
Harvard Business Review on **Corporate Strategy**	1429
Harvard Business Review on **Crisis Management**	2352
Harvard Business Review on **Culture and Change**	8369
Harvard Business Review on **Customer Relationship Management**	6994
Harvard Business Review on **Decision Making**	5572

To order, call 1-800-668-6780, or go online at www.HBSPress.org

To order, call 1-800-668-6780, or go online at www.HBSPress.org

Harvard Business Essentials

In the fast-paced world of business today, everyone needs a personal resource—a place to go for advice, coaching, background information, or answers. The Harvard Business Essentials series fits the bill. Concise and straightforward, these books provide highly practical advice for readers at all levels of experience. Whether you are a new manager interested in expanding your skills or an experienced executive looking to stay on top, these solution-oriented books give you the reliable tips and tools you need to improve your performance and get the job done. Harvard Business Essentials titles will quickly become your constant companions and trusted guides.

These books are priced at US$19.95, except as noted.
Price subject to change.

Title	Product #
Harvard Business Essentials: **Negotiation**	1113
Harvard Business Essentials: **Managing Creativity and Innovation**	1121
Harvard Business Essentials: **Managing Change and Transition**	8741
Harvard Business Essentials: **Hiring and Keeping the Best People**	875X
Harvard Business Essentials: **Finance for Managers**	8768
Harvard Business Essentials: **Business Communication**	113X
Harvard Business Essentials: **Manager's Toolkit ($24.95)**	2896
Harvard Business Essentials: **Managing Projects Large and Small**	3213
Harvard Business Essentials: **Creating Teams with an Edge**	290X
Harvard Business Essentials: **Entrepreneur's Toolkit**	4368
Harvard Business Essentials: **Coaching and Mentoring**	435X
Harvard Business Essentials: **Crisis Management**	4376
Harvard Business Essentials: **Time Management**	6336
Harvard Business Essentials: **Power, Influence, and Persuasion**	631X
Harvard Business Essentials: **Strategy**	6328

The Results-Driven Manager

The Results-Driven Manager series collects timely articles from *Harvard Management Update* and *Harvard Management Communication Letter* to help senior to middle managers sharpen their skills, increase their effectiveness, and gain a competitive edge. Presented in a concise, accessible format to save managers valuable time, these books offer authoritative insights and techniques for improving job performance and achieving immediate results.

These books are priced at US$14.95
Price subject to change.

Title	Product #
The Results-Driven Manager:	
Face-to-Face Communications for Clarity and Impact	3477
The Results-Driven Manager:	
Managing Yourself for the Career You Want	3469
The Results-Driven Manager:	
Presentations That Persuade and Motivate	3493
The Results-Driven Manager: **Teams That Click**	3507
The Results-Driven Manager:	
Winning Negotiations That Preserve Relationships	3485
The Results-Driven Manager: **Dealing with Difficult People**	6344
The Results-Driven Manager: **Taking Control of Your Time**	6352
The Results-Driven Manager: **Getting People on Board**	6360
The Results-Driven Manager:	
Motivating People for Improved Performance	7790
The Results-Driven Manager: **Becoming an Effective Leader**	7804
The Results-Driven Manager:	
Managing Change to Reduce Resistance	7812
The Results-Driven Manager:	
Hiring Smart for Competitive Advantage	9726
The Results-Driven Manager:	
Retaining Your Best People	9734
The Results-Driven Manager:	
Business Etiquette for the New Workplace	9742

How to Order

Harvard Business School Press publications are available worldwide from your local bookseller or online retailer.
You can also call

1-800-668-6780

Our product consultants are available to help you
8:00 a.m.–6:00 p.m., Monday–Friday, Eastern Time.
Outside the U.S. and Canada, call: 617-783-7450
Please call about special discounts for quantities greater than ten.

You can order online at

www.HBSPress.org